THE OPINION MAKERS

The Opinion Makers

An Insider Exposes the Truth
Behind the Polls

DAVID W. MOORE

BEACON PRESS   BOSTON

Beacon Press
25 Beacon Street
Boston, Massachusetts 02108-2892
www.beacon.org

Beacon Press books
are published under the auspices of
the Unitarian Universalist Association of Congregations.

11 10 09 08   8 7 6 5 4 3 2 1

This book is printed on acid-free paper that
meets the uncoated paper ANSI/NISO
specifications for permanence as revised in 1992.

Text design by Tag Savage at
Wilsted & Taylor Publishing Services

Library of Congress Cataloging-in-Publication Data

Moore, David W. (David William)
 The opinion makers : an insider exposes the truth behind the polls /
David W. Moore.
      p. cm.
 Includes bibliographical references and index.
 ISBN-13: 978-0-8070-4232-8 (hardcover : alk. paper)
 ISBN 0-8070-4232-3 (hardcover)
 1. Public opinion—United States. 2. Public opinion polls—United
States. 3. Election forecasting—United States. 4. Mass media—Political
aspects—United States. 5. Press and politics—United States. I. Title.

 HN90.P8M65 2008
 303.3'80973—dc22   2008015392

To Zelda

As the mass media have taken control over the polling profession, Gresham's law applies in full force . . . Poor quality drives out good quality.

DANIEL YANKELOVICH
founder of the Public Agenda Foundation
and author of *Coming to Public Judgment*

Despite mounting evidence that poll results can't be trusted, pundits and politicians continue to treat them with a reverence ancient Romans reserved for chicken entrails.

ARIANNA HUFFINGTON

The media do a terrible, terrible, terrible job with polls.

JIM CLIFTON
president and CEO of the Gallup Organization

CONTENTS

Pollsters under Attack

It's a tragic irony that one of the twentieth century's most cele-
brated social inventions, widely anticipated as a means of enhancing democracy, has turned out to do the opposite. When
in the mid-1930s George Gallup, Elmo Roper, and Archibald
Crossley unveiled their scientific method of conducting public
opinion polls, they expected that the people's voices would
now be heard not just at election time, but continuously.
And in one sense, they were absolutely prescient. These scientific pollsters launched an enterprise that has revolutionized the
way history is recorded. Before that time, historians "studied
nations in the aggregate, and gave us only the story of princes,
dynasties, sieges, and battles."[1] Now, with an archive of polls,
historians can study the people's history—detailed information about normal people's family lives, health, work habits,
leisure and travel activities, religious beliefs and behavior, living
arrangements, sexual activity, finances, experience with crime,
and of course their attitudes about anything from politics, religion, and sports to the latest social fads and entertainment
personalities. So profound is this new way of describing a
nation and its people that it has essentially defined the concept of mass public, by "shaping Americans' sense of them-

selves as individuals, members of communities, and citizens of a nation."[2]

A highly influential subset of these national polls record voters' preferences during election campaigns and measure the public's opinions on government policies. These two areas of measurement are important because of their clear relation to our country's democratic form of government, which—according to famed scholar and political scientist Harold D. Lasswell—depends on the vital interplay between government and the people. "Government acts upon public opinion, and public opinion acts openly and continually upon government,"[3] he wrote at the beginning of World War II. Six decades later, two other noted political scientists, Lawrence Jacobs and Robert Shapiro, made a similarly powerful point about the need for government to listen to the people, "Whether *democratic* government survives is not foreordained or guaranteed. What is critical is creating the expectation that substantial government responsiveness to public opinion is appropriate and necessary."[4]

Today, the areas of public opinion most relevant to the democratic process are measured almost exclusively by the major national media polls. Of course, they survey much more than voter preferences during election campaigns and ongoing attitudes toward public policy, and their contributions to our understanding of American culture are immense. Their performance in the area of democratic public opinion, however, has been less stellar. Indeed, it's in this area where their influence differs starkly from what was originally hoped.

FOR THIRTEEN YEARS I was employed by the Gallup Organization, with principal responsibilities initially as managing editor and subsequently as senior editor of the Gallup Poll. During that time, from March 1993 until April 2006, I shared the frustration that virtually all of the media pollsters felt as we took criticism from all quarters for supposed biases in our polls.

Some of the criticisms simply reflected a lack of under-standing about the nature of sampling. Indeed, the complaint pollsters hear most frequently from irate citizens is, "Why wasn't I polled?" Once, when I was being interviewed on radio, a caller demanded to know if his name was on a list the Gallup Poll would never call because he was a liberal (or conservative, I forget which). I was tempted to tell him I would check it out and get back to him, but I didn't. A good corporate representa-tive at the time, I didn't want to say anything that might even hint at a biased selection process. I reassured him that as far as was possible, every residential telephone number in the coun-try was eligible to be called, and that it was up to an apolitical computer to randomly select his household (at least if he lived in the forty-eight contiguous states; typically Gallup and other pollsters exclude Alaska and Hawaii because of their inconven-ient time zones and small populations).

Other criticisms, however, were more difficult to parry. One of the most intense periods of controversy occurred on Septem-ber 17, 2004, two weeks after the Republican National Conven-tion that nominated President George W. Bush for a second term. My news story on the Gallup website reported the results of the latest CNN/*USA Today*/Gallup poll with the headline, *Bush Bounce Keeps on Going.*[5] The "bounce" I was referring to was the surge in support that a presidential candidate typically gets after his party's nomination convention. Bush led by 3 per-centage points before the convention, but was up by 7 points af-terward. Ten days later, his lead had expanded an additional 6 points, and he led Senator John Kerry 55 percent to 42 percent.

The problem for anybody who cared even a smidgeon about the presidential race was that the day before my story was posted, Pew Research announced a dead heat between Bush and Kerry, and its headlines read, *Kerry Support Rebounds; Race Again Even.* The story noted that while Bush had surged to a 12-point lead after the Republican convention, the Bush bounce had suddenly disappeared.[6]

It's not unusual that polls conducted in roughly the same time period will conflict with each other, though such conflicts are still treated as aberrations. Usually, one can attribute the apparent contradictions to different interviewing dates or to dissimilar question wording. And, of course, there is always the possibility that one poll was just plain wrong, an explanation most likely to be heard if one of the polling organizations has a poor reputation anyway.

The conflicting results by Gallup and Pew, however, could not be explained away by any of the usual excuses. These were two titans in the polling industry, both highly respected among the news media, and neither poll could be immediately dismissed out of hand. Moreover, the dates of interviews for both surveys were almost identical, and there was no issue of question wording because each poll included the industry's standard question about which candidate a respondent would vote for if the election were held "today."

Press reaction to the conflicting results was explosive. The next day my colleague Jeff Jones, the Gallup Poll's managing editor, and I were buried by calls from reporters around the country demanding an explanation for the differences between the polls. Usually we referred such calls to Frank Newport, editor in chief, but on this day he was traveling. Nevertheless, he called from the airport in Detroit, asking how we had been dealing with the calls. He, too, had responded to several calls and was irritated that most reporters seemed to be critical of Gallup rather than Pew. Many in the press had criticized Gallup's tracking polls in the 1996 and 2000 presidential elections, claiming our results were "too volatile." Even Pew's Andrew Kohut had called them "loopy." This time it was Pew's numbers that were loopy, but Pew seemed to be getting a free ride.

Ultimately, the issue was resolved in the press when Scott Keeter, the director of surveys at Pew, and I agreed that the difference might well be attributed to "timing"—the Pew poll was conducted over a five-day period, Gallup's over three days, and it was a volatile period of campaigning. Prior to reaching the agreement with Keeter, I had already explained to one reporter my view of what went wrong. Before posing its presidential vote question, Pew had asked several questions about the news in general, including one about Bush's hotly debated National Guard service. In the final poll before the election, when all pollsters are trying to produce as accurate a prediction as possible, no one would dare precede the vote question with other general news questions for fear of distorting the results. In this case, because it wasn't the final preelection poll—which would be compared against actual election results to determine the polling organization's accuracy—Pew apparently didn't feel the need to be so cautious. But Pew's probing questions about Bush before the vote question may very well have prompted many respondents to think twice about saying they were going to vote for the president, and thus depressed his apparent support. That, at least, was the view at Gallup. As it turned out, the reporter mentioned none of that in his story, and instead accepted the timing excuse.[7]

Despite these and other polling conflicts during the 2004 presidential campaign, most of the polls, including Pew's and Gallup's, converged on a similar prediction of a slight Bush victory. But many observers were not impressed. No matter the agreement they had reached by Election Day, the polls had showed sharply divergent results during the campaign. The negative feelings about the preelection polls were exacerbated by the performance of the exit polls, which early on Election Night showed Kerry winning the presidency, only to be reversed sometime after midnight to show a Bush victory.

"Spectacularly stinko," said the *Raleigh (N.C.) News and Observer* in a blistering appraisal of the final preelection polls.[8] Noted journalist Christopher Hitchens said, "All I wanted [from the 2004 presidential election] . . . is a result that made the pollsters look stupid and it well exceeded my expectations in this respect."[9] "Junk!" is what Bill Wheatley, vice president of

NBC News, called the 2004 exit polls.[10] Jimmy Breslin, writing for *Newsday*, was more expansive. "If you want a poll on the Kerry-Bush race, sit down and make up your own," he said. "It is just as good as the monstrous frauds presented on television and the newspaper first pages."[11] Peter Coy of *Businessweek* took a broader view. "More and more Americans believe polls are unscientific, unreliable, biased, privacy-invading, and a waste of time," he wrote. "The reputation of pollsters is down around the abysmal level of that of journalists or used-car salesmen in the public's mind. Pollsters know this depressing news because they asked."[12] As we pollsters circled the wagons to fend off what we felt were irrational critics, we didn't have far to look for the principal culprits causing the ruckus. As the comic strip character Pogo said, "We have met the enemy, and he is us."

FOR YEARS, we pollsters have systematically misled the American people about the accuracy of our polls, claiming a degree of precision in assessing public opinion that is far removed from reality. We do acknowledge, of course, a "margin of error" associated with the size of our samples, that well-known "plus or minus 3 percentage points" phrase suggesting that our polling numbers are usually very close to what we would have measured had we interviewed every living adult in the country. And just to cover ourselves, we add the not-so-innocuous fine print: "In addition to sampling error, question wording and practical difficulties in conducting surveys can introduce error or bias into the findings of public opinion polls." This phrase would scare the bejesus out of poll users if they understood what it really means. In fact, when I included this phrase on a report to one of Gallup's bank clients, the astute contact at the bank insisted it be deleted. "It essentially says you can't trust any of the numbers," she said. "What good is a report like that?"

In practice, most poll users simply ignore the warning about additional "error or bias," much as confirmed smokers are undeterred by the health notice on the side of the cigarette pack. But unlike smokers, poll users can hardly be blamed; they ignore our warning because we pollsters ignore it. We treat our numbers not as though they are rough estimates of what the public is thinking, but rather as fairly precise reflections of reality. But look carefully at almost any set of polling results, and you will see large variations among highly reputable polling organizations.

The vagaries of polls continued into 2005 on such matters as Social Security, oil drilling in Alaska, stem cell research, a constitutional amendment to ban same-sex marriages, troop levels in Iraq, and of course the controversy over Terri Schiavo, the Florida woman in a vegetative state for more than fifteen years who became a symbol of the culture war in America. On all of these issues, different polls showed significantly varied results—large majorities in one direction or another, depending on how pollsters decided to measure opinion.

Similarly, the 2006 midterm predictions of the U.S. House vote by seven media polls showed little consensus. Democrats were expected to win the total popular vote nationwide by just 3 percentage points according to Pew, but by 20 points according to CNN. Also in the single-digit predictions were USA Today/Gallup and the ABC/Washington Post polls, whereas Fox, Time, and Newsweek predicted winning margins that averaged 15 points. The final vote count was close to 7 percent.

In 2007, after the Democrats' victory in the midterm elections, polls could not come to an agreement on whether the public favored Congress's passing a nonbinding resolution to oppose President Bush's troop surge or, separately, Congress's cutting off funding for the war in Iraq altogether. Some polls showed large majorities in favor, whereas others showed large majorities opposed. Polls also differed on whether Americans supported an extension of the State Children's Health Insurance Program, wanted immediate U.S. troop withdrawal from

Iraq, or agreed with General Petraeus's report on the performance of the troop surge in Iraq.

The 2008 presidential campaign season began no better. Polls in all the early contests were far off the mark, the most notable being those in the New Hampshire Democratic Primary, which predicted a victory for Barack Obama by an average margin of 8 percentage points. He lost by 2 points, causing extreme consternation among pollsters and political observers alike. In South Carolina, the polls' errors were even greater, correctly predicting Obama to win but by a margin that was only half the actual outcome. Poll results in Iowa and Nevada were hardly better. Looking ahead to Super Tuesday, Frank Rich of the *New York Times* wrote, "As Tuesday's vote looms, all that's certain is that today's pollsters and pundits have so far gotten almost everything wrong."[13] The disastrous performance of the polls in the early part of the primary season followed an abominable performance in the preprimary period. For months, polls reported a "solid" lead for Hillary Clinton among the national primary electorate, so solid that it evaporated after the very first contest, the Iowa primary. Rudy Giuliani was consistently treated as the national Republican frontrunner, even though he trailed in all of the early contests and was dethroned from his exalted status within the first week of actual voting, never to recover.

These and similar examples raise serious doubts about the utility of polls. Can we trust any of their findings to represent what people are really thinking? What does it mean when they present conflicting numbers during election campaigns, and between elections when reporting on public policy matters? How biased are the polls? And just whose interests do they serve?

The national media polls referred to in this book include thirteen polling organizations. Probably the four most influential are the two affiliated with the most prestigious general newspapers in the country: the *New York Times*/CBS News poll

and the *Washington Post*/ABC News poll.[14] The other two polls
in this group are Pew Research and *USA Today*/Gallup. These
four organizations are more likely than others to see their results
picked up by news media organizations for further dissemina-
tion, in part because of their reputations and in part because of
the relative frequency of their polling. Though it's difficult to
say which of the top four is the most influential, it's clear that,
combined, these four polls overwhelmingly shape the country's
public opinion environment. The other media polls mentioned
in this book are those by CNN, NBC/*Wall Street Journal, Time,
Newsweek,* the Associated Press/Ipsos, the *Los Angeles Times,*
Fox, John Zogby (often with Reuters), and Harris Interactive
(with different media organizations, but no regular partner). All
of these organizations poll less frequently or have no daily national print partner. There is nothing in this classification that
suggests the quality of the polls is less among the second group
of polls than in the first group.

IN THIS BOOK, I focus on how these polls assess and influence
the two most important areas of democratic public opinion:
voters' preferences during an election campaign and public attitudes about government policies. For many people, public
opinion has become whatever the major media polls say it is.
My take is a bit different. I accept the principle that polls can
measure public opinion, but only if they tell the truth about the
public. Unfortunately, they don't. Instead, media polls give us
distorted readings of the electoral climate, manufacture a false
public consensus on policy issues, and in the process undermine American democracy.

CHAPTER ONE

Iraq and the Polls—
The Myth of War Support

She referred to herself as "a tall redhead with a foreign accent," but to the audience her physical characteristics and her considerable humor were her least important attributes. She came to the meeting a "sworn enemy" of pollsters, in their view an articulate but misguided soul who had started a campaign to end all polling, which she dubbed on her website a "Partnership for a Poll-Free America." She wanted the public to take pollsters to court and put them out of business. The notion that pollsters are listening to the vox populi is pathological, she argued, noting "the ludicrousness of basing anything on increasingly inaccurate opinion polls, with their plummeting response rates, laughably small samplings and precision-flouting margins of error."[1]

Because of her antipathy to their profession, the pollsters had invited her to address the 2003 annual meeting of the American Association for Public Opinion Research, the foremost professional organization of survey research practitioners and scholars in the country. She had just finished her speech to the people she wanted to see unemployed, and the first respondent to her arguments was Rich Morin, who then was the polling director of the *Washington Post*.

"There are actually two Arianna Huffingtons," Morin told

the audience as he nodded toward the guest speaker. There was the "delightful, witty, charming, and perceptive" Arianna, with whom he and several other members of the association had dined earlier; and there was the public persona Arianna, the one with her website and column and public appearances: "the shrieking pundit from hell!" Laughter erupted from the audience, as well as from Huffington and the other respondents on the dais.[2]

In her speech to the pollsters, however, Huffington was less a shrieking pundit and more a conciliator, urging members to find a way "to put the real problems the country is facing" high on the political agenda. Ideally, she argued, polls would help political leaders to understand what the public wants, but in actual practice, polls do not represent what the public is really thinking. She excoriated former President Bill Clinton for running a poll-driven presidency, and she lambasted President George W. Bush for allowing public opinion polls to lead him into war. She reiterated her contention, developed earlier on her website, that "the greatest threat to the body politic is that polls turn political leaders into slavish followers of the most shallow reading of the electorate's whims and wishes."[3]

As it turns out, she was wrong about Bush's following opinion polls into war. We now know that Bush and his major advisors were intent on invading Iraq from the beginning of his presidency, and that the decision to do so was made in the immediate aftermath of the 9/11 attacks. Public opinion had no influence on that decision. But the public's apparently positive response to the Bush administration's campaign for war did, arguably, influence many others in the country, especially many Democratic political leaders in Congress, who were intimidated by public opinion into voting for war despite their reservations about attacking a country that had not directly threatened the United States.

In the months leading up to the U.S. invasion of Iraq, all the major media polls appeared to show substantial public support for the war.[4] Within a week of the invasion, the polls reported approval running ahead of disapproval 2-to-1 or better. The ABC/*Washington Post* poll reported 71 percent of Americans in favor, 27 percent opposed. The NBC/*Wall Street Journal* poll reported 65 percent in favor, 30 percent opposed. The CNN/*USA Today*/Gallup poll reported a similar split, 64 percent to 33 percent. *Newsweek* said it was 70 percent to 24 percent.

Much research suggests that when large majorities of the public are perceived in favor of certain policies, people with different opinions tend to suppress their own views. As scholar Elizabeth Noelle-Neumann, notes:

> If people believe that their opinion is part of a consensus, they have the confidence to speak out in both private and public discussions, displaying their convictions with buttons and car stickers, for example, but also by the clothes they wear and other publicly visible symbols. Conversely, when people feel that they are in the minority, they become cautious and silent, thus reinforcing the impression of weakness, until the apparently weaker side disappears completely except for a hard core that holds on to its previous values, or until the opinion becomes taboo.[5]

Although polls suggested that hard-core opponents of the war included at least a quarter of the American public, it's noteworthy that few demonstrations against the war occurred in the United States until years later, after polls showed a majority of Americans saying the war was a mistake.

The news media also hopped onto the war bandwagon, giving biased coverage in favor of policies that appeared to be supported by large majorities of Americans and limiting coverage of dissenting opinions. Two years after the start of the Iraq war, the *New York Times* published a startling admission: that leading up to the invasion, it had failed its readers by slanting its news very heavily in favor of the Bush administration's position, giving less than one-tenth of its coverage to dissenting views.

The *Washington Post* made a similar admission. Though the *Times* and the *Post* apologized for their behavior, they were not alone in their biased coverage. The rush to war was aided and abetted by virtually all of the major news media organizations, which mostly emulated the two most prestigious national newspapers.[6]

This climate of public opinion in favor of the war apparently also intimidated Democratic members of Congress, especially those who had any thoughts of running for president. In the U.S. House, not traditionally a launch pad for presidential candidates, Democrats voting against the resolution that gave Bush the authority to invade Iraq outnumbered Democrats voting for it 126 to 81 (61 percent to 39 percent). But in the U.S. Senate, a source of many hopeful presidential candidates, 29 of the 50 Democrats casting votes supported the war resolution, including several senators who had been mentioned as possible presidential candidates or who later ran for president: Joe Biden, Hillary Clinton, Tom Daschle, Chris Dodd, Evan Bayh, John Edwards, John Kerry, and Dianne Feinstein. The new Senate majority leader in 2007, Harry Reid, also voted for the resolution, though—like the others—he later opposed the war. Had these nine senators ignored public opinion polls and voted to oppose the war in March 2003, the Senate vote among Democrats would have approximated the House vote among Democrats—30 to 20 votes (60 percent to 40 percent).

Those 20 Democratic votes in favor of the resolution, along with the votes of 48 of the 49 Republican senators, would have ensured passage even had the nine Democratic senators not been intimidated by the polls. Still, the supportive votes by those nine senators, along with biased media coverage and suppression of war dissent, supported Arianna Huffington's criticisms. Polls turn political leaders and (though she didn't mention it) the news media "into slavish followers of the most shallow reading of the electorate's whims and wishes."

Contrary to media reports on that climate of war opinion,

three CNN/*USA Today*/Gallup polls conducted in the months leading up to the war and immediately after the war began showed that a majority of Americans were not calling for war.[7] The second of these polls, conducted in February 2003, about a month before the invasion, showed an evenly divided public —about three in ten Americans wanted the United States to attack Iraq, three in ten were opposed, and four in ten *did not care one way or the other.* That this divided state of public opinion was not measured by the other media polls and that neither CNN, *USA Today,* nor Gallup emphasized the public's ambivalence about the war reveals much about the way that media polls manufacture public opinion for their own purposes.

THE REASON THAT all the polling organizations missed the actual split in public opinion on Iraq is that pollsters typically insist on asking policy questions of everyone in their sample, regardless of whether the people know or care anything about the issue. And respondents happily go along with the "don't ask, don't tell" game that we pollsters play—we don't ask them, and they don't tell us, how little they know or care about an issue. That way, we end up with a "public opinion" that is more interesting to report than one that acknowledges the truth of substantial public ignorance and apathy.

This issue had troubled me ever since I joined the Gallup Organization. By the time of the Iraq war, my Gallup colleague Jeff Jones, who by then was the managing editor, and I, the senior editor, had been running a series of experiments designed to give more meaning to our poll findings. We were given limited space to run the experiments, and this was one of those times when we were able to include a special follow-up question to test the firmness of people's views.

In the February 2003 poll, we asked a standard version of the question that all the other pollsters asked, "Would you favor or oppose sending American ground troops to the Persian

Gulf in an attempt to remove Saddam Hussein from power in Iraq?" And like the other polls, we found a substantial majority in favor of the war—59 percent to 38 percent, a 21-point margin. Only 3 percent said they did not have an opinion. We followed up that question with another, which essentially asked if people really cared that their opinion might prevail. And the results here revealed a very different public.

To people who said they favored the war, we asked if they would be upset if the government did not send troops to Iraq. And to people who opposed the war, we asked if they would be upset if the government did send troops. More than half of the supposed supporters and a fifth of the opponents said they would *not* be upset if their opinions were ignored. The net result is that 29 percent of Americans actually supported the war and said they would be upset if it didn't come about, whereas 30 percent were opposed to the war and said they would be upset if it did occur. An additional 38 percent, who had expressed an opinion either for or against the proposed invasion, said they would not be upset if the government did the opposite of what they had just favored. Add to this number the 3 percent who initially expressed no opinion, and that makes 41 percent who didn't care one way or the other (see fig. 1).

These results from the follow-up question reveal the absurdity of much public opinion polling. A democracy is supposed to represent, or at least take into account, the "will" of the people, not the uncaring, unreflective, top-of-mind responses many people give to pollsters. If people don't care that the views they tell pollsters are ignored by their political leaders, then it hardly makes sense for pollsters to treat such responses as the Holy Grail. Yet, typically we do, making no distinction between those who express deeply held views and those who have hardly, if at all, thought about an issue.

It is useful here to differentiate between "directive" and "permissive" opinion. People who have an opinion about the war and care that their political leaders listen to it can be

FIGURE 1

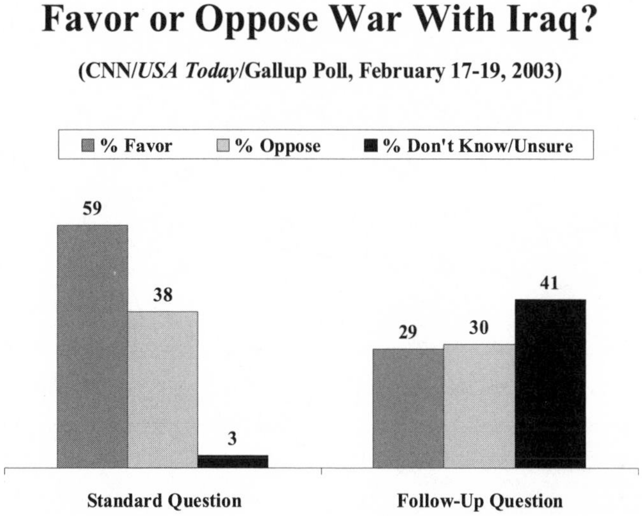

Favor or Oppose War With Iraq?

(CNN/*USA Today*/Gallup Poll, February 17-19, 2003)

| ▨ % Favor | ☐ % Oppose | ■ % Don't Know/Unsure |

59

38

41

29   30

3

Standard Question   Follow-Up Question

viewed as having a "directive" opinion, because they implicitly want to direct their leaders to follow it. Our poll showed that 59 percent of Americans had a directive opinion in February 2003, but were evenly divided over the war, with 29 percent in favor and 30 percent against. The other 41 percent can be viewed as having a "permissive" opinion, because they didn't care if their views were followed or not, or they expressed no preference one way or the other. Essentially, they were permitting their representatives to make the crucial judgment, presumably on behalf of the citizens as a whole. After all, that's the reason citizens elect legislators and governors and presidents, so they will take the time to evaluate what policies are in the best interests of the public. Many people simply don't have time to consider all of the facts surrounding an issue and come up with a good decision as to how best to proceed.

What our polling results meant in 2003 was that a public consensus existed either *for* going to war or for *not* going to war. Seventy percent would have been content with invading Iraq (the 41 percent who didn't care plus the 29 percent who supported the war and would have been upset if it hadn't occurred), and 71 percent would have been content with *not* going to war (the 41 percent who didn't care plus the 30 percent who opposed the invasion and said they would be upset if it did occur). It was up to the elected leaders to make the call. Today, numerous pundits argue that the American people were partly responsible for going to war with Iraq because they gave overwhelming support for it. That simply isn't true. Maybe people should be held accountable because they *tolerated* the invasion, but the truth is that there was no majority of Americans *calling* for the United States to invade Iraq. Indeed, as many people opposed the war as supported it, with a major segment of the population "permitting" government officials to do whatever they thought best.

After the war began, most polls showed a surge of public support for the effort. A CNN/*USA Today*/Gallup poll conducted about three weeks after the invasion began found 68 percent who favored the war and 28 percent opposed. But the follow-up question on permissive versus directive opinions revealed that just 35 percent of Americans wanted the war to happen, 24 percent did not, and 41 percent didn't care one way or the other. The notion that the public "rallied around the flag" after the war began is a distortion of what really happened: about a third of Americans actually supported the war after it was launched, whereas a plurality of Americans still didn't care. Actual support increased by just a few percentage points, and opposition dropped by about the same magnitude. Thus, among those who did care about their opinions, the ones favoring the war outnumbered those opposing it by about 11 percentage points.

HOW IMPORTANT IS IT that the public didn't support the war before it was launched but was in fact evenly divided over it? Very important. Though it is clear now that the Bush administration was intent on going to war regardless of public opinion or congressional support, administration officials still used public opinion polls to mute criticisms and to help justify its actions. The fact that a large majority of the public appeared to support the war was a major element of the political climate that led to the actual invasion of Iraq, with the implicit message that public support at least partly justified the war.

An unusual reaction against this notion that public opinion can be used to justify policy decisions came from a prominent pollster in December 2001, barely three months after the terrorist attacks in New York City and Washington, D.C. Humphrey Taylor, chairman of the Harris Poll, wrote to the *New York Times*[8] expressing his agreement with recent articles by Anthony Lewis[9] and William Safire,[10] which contained scathing criticisms of the Bush administration's new rules on the way suspected terrorists could be treated and tried. Lewis noted that the military tribunal order established special military courts to try the terrorists, but they were to have more relaxed standards of what could be admitted as evidence than is allowed in either the U.S. civil or military courts, easier standards for conviction, no judicial review, and no assurance for defendants of choosing their own attorneys, among other provisions. Safire referred to the order as "the sudden seizure of power, bypassing all constitutional checks and balances," and suggested that "cooler heads" in the government were beginning to recognize that it was "more than a bit excessive."

Taylor was concerned because administration supporters had rebutted the two *New York Times* columnists by quoting polls, including his own, "which show that [the Bush administration's] actions and proposals enjoy the support of large majorities of the public." He didn't deny the poll results or suggest they might constitute a misreading of the public will, but instead argued that they should not be used to defend bad policy. "In times of war and national emergencies—from John Adams's Sedition Act to Franklin D. Roosevelt's rounding up of Japanese Americans—most people have probably approved of draconian measures that we later came to regret," Taylor wrote. "Our legislators should certainly be well informed about public opinion. But they should make up their own minds on the merits of the case, with one eye on how history will judge them." And he had a point, since numerous polls over the years have shown that, in general, a majority of Americans do not support the Bill of Rights when the freedoms it protects are presented as hypothetical situations. In fact, Safire referred to polls showing "terrorized Americans willing to subvert our Constitution to hold Soviet-style secret military trials. No presumption of innocence; no independent juries; no right to choice of counsel; no appeal to civilian judges." But such views, however widespread among the people, are not considered justification for violating the Constitution.

Apart from such use of polls, my concern was more basic: Did the polls about military tribunals even give us an accurate reading of what the public really wanted to happen? Gallup addressed the issue[11] by asking the public two questions, the first one being, "If suspected terrorists are captured and put on trial, do you think they should be tried by an international court or by U.S. authorities?" For people who know nothing about international law or what treaties the United States has signed or what U.S. policy is toward other nations that capture U.S. citizens in combat, why wouldn't they choose "U.S. authorities"? And indeed a majority did, 56 percent to 41 percent. The next question asked that if suspected terrorists were to be tried in the United States, would respondents rather see that happen "in a regular court of law in which evidence would be presented in a public trial, or a military tribunal in which U.S. officers would examine evidence in secret hearings?" Since the choice was for terrorists to be tried by a regular court or a military tribunal, it would seem logical that terrorists, who constituted the enemy in a military "war against terrorism," should be tried by a military tribunal. Sure enough, a majority took that position,

53 percent to 42 percent. Did all the respondents in the poll pay close attention to the whole question and realize that the military tribunal would accept evidence only in secret hearings, or did they just get the idea that there were military prisoners who would be tried in military courts? Sometimes, we pollsters pack a lot of meaningful information into our questions, and foolishly expect that the respondents will absorb every nuance.

My assumption was that for many people these results reflected a top-of-mind response, in large part influenced by the way the question was phrased. If we had asked all the respondents whether they cared if their choice was the one the government followed, I suspected that many would readily admit they didn't really care. I was never able to test that suspicion on the military tribunal questions, but eventually Gallup did measure public commitment to opinions on a similar matter—the closing of the prison in Guantanamo Bay.

Alleged Public Support for "Gitmo"

In the summer of 2005, a major controversy arose over the U.S. imprisonment of suspected terrorists at Guantanamo Bay in Cuba—something that had been authorized four years earlier, but now, in the aftermath of the Abu Ghraib scandal, was receiving new attention. The controversy over the Guantanamo prison received a great deal of press attention, but it was still just one of many public policy issues in the news. If we pollsters were going to ask people what the government should do about the facility, at least we ought to know how much, if anything, they knew about it. But, of course, that was not what the media wanted to find out, because the public's lack of attention to the issue might call into question the validity of any opinions we were going to measure. So, in June of that year, we didn't ask what people knew. Instead, we gave *them* information, to be sure they would feel they knew enough about the issue to answer us:[12] "As you know, since 2001, the United States has held

people from other countries who are suspected of being terrorists at a detention facility in Guantanamo Bay in Cuba." This is
at best a bland presentation of a rather controversial situation,
where the issues were possible torture of prisoners and U.S. violation of the Geneva Convention on handling prisoners captured during war. We used phrasing to encourage people to
respond, even though they might feel they didn't know enough
to comment: "Based on what you have heard or read, do you
think the U.S. should continue to operate this facility, or do
you think the U.S. should close this facility and transfer the
prisoners to other facilities?" Essentially, we asked for their
best guess.

Without knowing how many people even knew about the
prison at Guantanamo Bay, or what proportion might know
about the controversy over the lack of safeguards required by
the Geneva Convention or any of the other details, Gallup
could report that a majority of Americans, 58 percent, supported the Bush administration's continued operation of the
prison facility, 36 percent were opposed, and only 6 percent
were unsure.

For people who had not followed the news on these matters, why shouldn't they give positive responses? The prison, after all, was for suspected terrorists—Gallup just told them that.
And Americans' immediate reaction to government activity
on behalf of the national defense is understandably positive;
our government, after all, wouldn't mistreat prisoners. The
likely truth, of course, was that relatively few people had heard
of the Guantanamo Bay prison, and that even among those who
had, most were undoubtedly ignorant of what was actually happening there. The accurate report on public opinion should
have included, at the very least, how few people were truly informed about the issue, instead of results that indicated a solid
majority of the American people in support of the policy.

Two years later, Gallup finally included that issue as part
of the series of experiments that Jeff Jones and I had initiated

(although by that time I had left Gallup, and it was only Jones who continued with that effort). The new question was different from the old one in two aspects. It was not preceded by any explanation about the prison—no feeding of information so respondents would know what the issue was about. (There was no question that asked how much respondents actually knew about the prison.) And it asked only whether the prison should be closed or not, rather than whether the government should continue to operate it or close it (a minor wording difference with the original question): "Do you think the United States should—or should not—close the prison at the Guantanamo Bay military base in Cuba?" Not surprisingly, more people volunteered they didn't have an opinion (13 percent) in 2007 than did so in 2005 (6 percent) when they were fed some information. Nevertheless, among those offering an opinion, the public was divided about the same in 2007 as it had been earlier—53 percent against closing the base to 33 percent in favor of it, a margin only two points smaller than the one in 2005 (see fig. 2).

The big revelation came when pollsters asked the follow-up question: whether the respondent would be upset if the government did the opposite of what he or she had just said. A majority, 52 percent, indicated they did not care (would not be "upset") one way or the other. The rest were divided, with 28 percent opposed to closing the base, and 19 percent in favor.

Instead of a 20-point margin between the two sides, the follow-up question found only a 9-point margin, with a majority not caring one way or the other. This was a picture of public opinion very different from the one Gallup reported in 2005 and very different from the Harris polls that showed majority support for the special military tribunal procedures announced by the Bush administration in 2001. In reality, large numbers of people simply had not thought about the issue and didn't have opinions that they wanted the government to follow.

If "forced" to give an opinion in a survey, many respondents

FIGURE 2

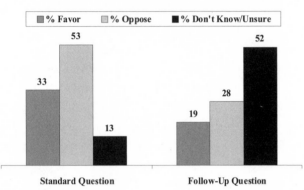

Favor or Oppose Closing Prison at Guantanamo Bay in Cuba?

(*USA Today*/Gallup Poll, July 6-8, 2007)

| ■ % Favor | □ % Oppose | ■ % Don't Know/Unsure |

Standard Question   Follow-Up Question

will indulge the interviewers and select a response that seems logical on the surface. But that choice hardly qualifies as a view that elected officials should treat with deference—especially when large numbers of respondents say immediately after expressing their view that they don't care whether or not it prevails.

Why NOT an Antimissile Shield?

Even with the follow-up question, the results about Guantanamo prison probably overestimated the number of people who actually had a developed opinion on the issue. The original question was in a "forced choice" format, which means respondents were offered only two options. If the respondents felt they didn't know enough about the issue to have an opinion, they had to volunteer that information. Sometimes, however, a policy question explicitly offers a "don't know" option and, in those cases, the percentage of people who acknowledge not having an opinion is always much higher than when people have to volunteer that information.

That was the case with a poll in April 2002, when Jeff Jones and I included two questions on antimissile defense that had been asked in previous years.[13] One included an explicit option for the respondent to indicate "don't know," and it was asked of half the sample of respondents. The other question was in a format that offered no options other than support or opposition, and it was asked of the other half of the sample.

At the time, news reports indicated that the Bush administration was getting ready to withdraw from the 1972 Anti-Ballistic Missile Treaty signed by the United States and the Soviet Union, in order to undertake development of systems that were banned by that treaty. (The official withdrawal occurred on June 13, 2002). Both poll questions began by telling the respondents, "Recently there has been some discussion about the possibility of the United States building a defense system against nuclear missiles." They then asked, "Do you think the government should or should not spend the money that would be necessary to build such a system?" One question stopped there, whereas the other added, "Or are you unsure?"

The standard question found more than 2-to-1 support for building an antimissile system, 64 percent to 30 percent. Just 6 percent of respondents volunteered they didn't know. For people who had no knowledge about the proposed system—how much it would cost, whether it would work, and what the political implications might be—the answer was a no-brainer. Who wouldn't say yes to a system that promised defense against nuclear missiles?

The second question, asked of people who had not been asked the forced-choice format question, found a third of respondents (33 percent) willing to say they were unsure. The rest favored building an antimissile system 47 percent to 20 percent. When these respondents were then asked whether they would

FIGURE 3

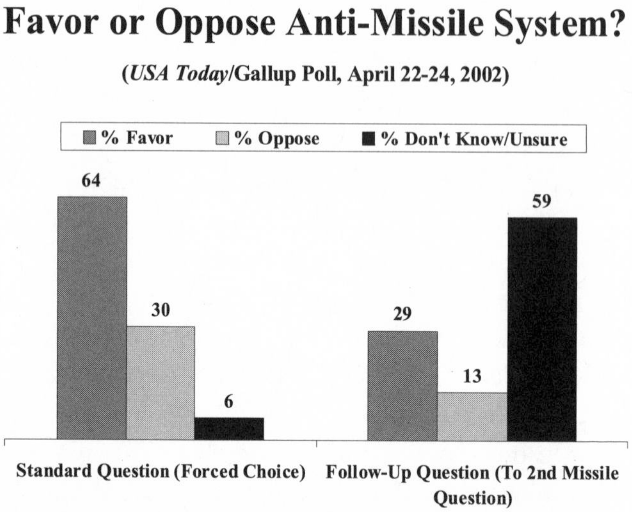

Favor or Oppose Anti-Missile System?

(*USA Today*/Gallup Poll, April 22-24, 2002)

| ■ % Favor | □ % Oppose | ■ % Don't Know/Unsure |

Standard Question (Forced Choice)   Follow-Up Question (To 2nd Missile Question)

be upset if the government did the opposite of what they had just said, 29 percent favored the system (and would be upset if it were not funded), 13 percent were opposed (and would be upset if it were built), with 59 percent indicating either that they did not have an opinion or didn't care what the government did (see fig. 3).[14]

The contrast in results between the two approaches to measuring public opinion on this issue provides a telling insight into what is wrong with standard polling methods. In both cases, there is 2-to-1 support for the antimissile system, but the reported proportion of the public that is engaged in the issue differs significantly in the two approaches. The standard question portrays virtually the entire public as engaged and well informed, with only 6 percent declining to express an opinion. But when people are first offered the option of saying they are unsure—as they were in the second question—and are then asked if they care whether their opinion is followed by the government, we find a substantial majority of the public neither engaged in nor well informed about the issue.

Two years earlier, several polling organizations asked about the antimissile program and produced results that differed according to how they phrased the questions. Most found initial support, but when they read negative information about the program—including its $60 billion cost, its low likelihood of working, and the need to break a thirty-year-old treaty with Russia if development was to proceed—support dropped precipitously.[15] The ease with which opinions could be manipulated suggests how superficial they really were.

IT'S CLEAR THAT on three of the most militarily aggressive policies of the twenty-first century to date, the major media polls have erroneously described: a saber-rattling public in the lead-up to the Iraq war, substantial majorities of Americans in favor of the draconian steps taken by the Bush administration to deprive suspected terrorists of their rights under the U.S. Constitution and the Geneva Convention, and widespread support for the construction of an antimissile system. All of these poll measures included large numbers of people, at least four in ten, who in fact had no emotional or intellectual commitment to the views they put forth. They were just as ready to see an outcome opposite to the one they chose. Once these people are correctly classified, the resulting picture of public opinion is substantially different from the portrayal provided by the media pollsters.

Still, whether accurate pictures of public opinion would have prevented the war in Iraq or given our political leaders second thoughts about supporting the missile shield and the prison at Guantanamo Bay are only of tangential concern. My major worry is with the broader implications of mismeasuring the public will—that on all sorts of issues, the media polls continually and systematically distort public opinion, with severe consequences for us all.

CHAPTER TWO

Manufacturing Public Opinion

In March 1993, when I joined the Gallup Organization as a vice president and managing editor of the Gallup Poll, I quickly realized that my preconceptions about the nature of public opinion, at least as measured by the news media polls, were inaccurate. I discovered that it wasn't by accident or inattention that the media manufacture public opinion based on the myth of an all-knowing, rational, and fully engaged public. To the contrary, it appears as though all of the media polls have an unwavering commitment to such a mythological public, perhaps feeling that only such an attuned citizenry can justify the beat of public opinion. If a large proportion of Americans has no real opinion on an issue, most media organizations might dismiss the poll results as having no news value. And if that happened on a regular basis, the whole enterprise of media polls could be jeopardized.

The hard truth is that on most policy issues, large proportions of the public know or care little about the specifics, and thus have developed no meaningful opinion about them. But news media polls typically gloss over public ignorance and apathy, and instead, through the use of forced-choice questions, squeeze some type of answer out of virtually all respondents—

with typically only a small percentage who volunteer that they know too little to express an opinion. The media then treat these responses as though they represent serious judgments, rather than the superficial notions that they really are. The net result is that frequently the media distort or completely mischaracterize what the American public is really thinking.

PRIOR TO JOINING Gallup I had been a professor at the University of New Hampshire in the political science department, teaching courses on American government that included public opinion, elections, and the news media. In 1975, I started conducting statewide telephone polls as part of class exercises in courses on public opinion and elections, and then expanded the effort to work with the local news media. Eventually, I helped establish the university's Survey Center and also wrote a book about national polling.[1] While researching the book, I interviewed Alec Gallup, whose father, the late George Gallup, was the "father" of modern media polling. I was startled to receive a telephone call from him several months after the book was published, asking if I could recommend anyone who might be qualified and interested in joining the Gallup Poll as the managing editor. I suggested several names, but no sooner did I utter a name than he rejected it. He asked me to think about it some more and give him a call the following week. When I called back and tentatively suggested my own name, he laughed and said he had hoped I would be interested but had been unwilling to ask me directly because he assumed many academics would disdain working in the commercial world.

As it turns out, the most startling adjustment I had to make after joining Gallup wasn't with commercial polling—something with which I was already familiar from my work at the Survey Center—but with something more basic. In late 1988, four years after George Gallup's death and a year after his widow's death, a small research company from Lincoln, Nebraska, called Selection Research Inc. (SRI) bought the Gallup Organization and fundamentally transformed the company from what it was when Gallup was alive. Gallup's two sons, Alec and George Jr., remained with the new Gallup Organization, but more as figureheads than as executives with real power. By that time, the Gallup Poll's visibility had declined considerably from its heyday—the 1950s to the 1970s, when there was only one other major polling organization, Louis Harris and Associates. By the beginning of the 1980s, just a few years before Gallup died, the three television networks had all created their own polls, each partnering with a major newspaper—ABC with the *Washington Post,* CBS with the *New York Times,* and NBC with the *Wall Street Journal* (after a brief partnership with the Associated Press). Other national polls emerged as well, including the *Los Angeles Times* poll and occasional polls by *Time* and *Newsweek* magazines (the latter conducted by Gallup until 1993).

By the time SRI bought the Gallup Organization, after the 1988 presidential election, the Gallup poll had all but disappeared from most national news stories. Few major newspapers continued to subscribe to Gallup's polling service, because most newspapers got their poll results for free, recycled from the newspapers and television networks that conducted their own polls. The company was founded by Donald O. Clifton, a psychology professor at the University of Nebraska in Lincoln, who designed questions that would help match people's personality characteristics (which he termed "strengths," apparently because it had greater sales appeal) with specific types of jobs. Based on his research, he eventually founded SRI to help other companies hire employees. In 1988, when SRI acquired Gallup, it was like one guppy eating another—the annual revenues from SRI were only slightly larger than the annual revenues from Gallup (around the $12 million to $15 million range). Today, Gallup's revenues exceed $200 million.

Among Clifton's four children was one son, Jim, who became president of the new Gallup Organization. Perhaps his most brilliant move came shortly after he took over as Gallup's "chief salesman" (his characterization, at least early on in his tenure, before he moved to Washington, D.C.), when he was attending the People's Choice Awards program in Los Angeles. Unlike the Academy Awards or Golden Globe Awards, the winners in the People's Choice Awards program were chosen based on Gallup polls. Typically each year a Gallup representative would go on camera to give a brief explanation of the polling methods. On awards night sometime after the acquisition of the Gallup Organization, Jim Clifton was in the green room, along with Ted Turner and his wife-to-be, Jane Fonda. Though Turner and Fonda seemed oblivious to others around them, that didn't prevent Clifton from interrupting them to suggest to Turner that CNN and Gallup form a polling partnership. Turner immediately declined, saying CNN couldn't afford it, but Clifton countered that Turner didn't even know how much it would cost. After some back-and-forth, Turner told Clifton to contact Ed Turner (no relation to Ted Turner) at CNN and talk to him about the idea. Clifton did, and the result was that CNN and Gallup, along with *USA Today* (CNN's occasional polling partner until then), formed a one-year partnership to conduct polls during the 1992 presidential election year. It was an ideal arrangement for all three organizations. Gallup was finally back in the news, because its poll results were immediately published on CNN and in *USA Today*. And the two media organizations benefited from the credibility of the Gallup poll. The cooperation among the three partners worked well during the campaign, and by the time I arrived four months after the presidential election the partnership had been renewed in a multiyear contract.

It quickly became clear to me that however much Gallup was billed as an equal partner with the two media organizations, it was CNN and *USA Today* that for all practical purposes determined which questions would be asked. Technically, Gallup had the final say on any wording and could also, if it chose to exercise this option, prevent any question from being asked. In practice, the polling representatives at the two media organizations would propose the topics for each new poll and the specific questions, which generally were chosen to correspond with the news stories being reported by their respective organizations. Gallup would invariably go along.

The major adjustment that I had to make came in the first several weeks, as I became aware that our polling partners would systematically skirt around the big white elephant of public ignorance, instead asking questions about complex issues without first ascertaining whether the respondents had any knowledge of the subject matter. This was a practice that I knew could produce highly distorted pictures of public opinion.

About a decade and a half earlier, I had published an article in *Foreign Policy* that showed many polls at the time to be exaggerating public support for a new arms treaty with the Soviet Union.[2] Between November 1977 and November 1978, several polls conducted by Louis Harris and Associates and, separately, by NBC News and the Associated Press all found support in the 67 percent to 77 percent range for such a treaty. Each of those polls used the standard forced-choice format, which asks respondents for their opinion but doesn't offer an "unsure" option. Also conducted in the same time period, however, were two Roper polls that asked for opinions on a new arms treaty but offered as an option: "Or haven't you been paying much attention?" Support for the arms treaty registered at just above 40 percent. The contrast with the much higher percentages reported by the other polls suggested that many people facing a forced-choice format will come up with a response even though they really don't have an opinion. In this case, it sounded good to have a new "strategic arms limitation" treaty, even if people didn't know what it might mean, so the unsure respondents said they supported it rather than volunteer that they didn't know enough to say. The Roper polls showed that, contrary to the findings of the Harris and NBC polls, the Carter administration couldn't count on a supportive public in any battle to ratify a new treaty with the Soviet Union. Instead, most people either didn't know the issues involved or hadn't made up their minds and were thus subject to persuasion by either side.

The lesson I learned is that people tend to be accommodating when they answer polls. If we pollsters want them to guess at an answer, they will. If we want them to admit when they don't know enough to offer an opinion, most will do that, too. Yet even when given an "unsure" option, a few people will persist in answering questions when they know nothing about the topic—a point illustrated by George Bishop and his colleagues at the University of Cincinnati with a 1986 poll that found a third of respondents expressing an opinion about a nonexistent Public Affairs Act.[3]

Still, that was not really news. In his classic book on public opinion published years earlier, the late V.O. Key recounted how a "waggish" Los Angeles reporter included a question on a survey that asked if respondents thought "the Mann Act deters or helps the cause of organized labor." The Mann Act prohibited white slavery (forced prostitution) and banned the interstate transport of females for "immoral purposes." It had nothing to do with organized labor, but that fact was lost on the vast majority of respondents, who nevertheless offered their opinion. Just 12 percent knew enough to recognize they were being spoofed. Though the experiment was designed to show the flaws of polls, Key wrote that "all it demonstrated was that only a fool would ask such a question in such a form with the expectation that it would yield anything of utility."[4] Yet that's essentially the form of most questions that media pollsters ask today.

Although media pollsters rarely, if ever, deliberately trick their respondents, they all too frequently include questions about arcane issues without trying to measure how much people know about the subject. That's what struck me as most surprising in my early days of working with the Gallup Poll. During my first few weeks on the job, I observed and participated in the design of several questionnaires, which included whether people supported or opposed President Clinton's economic plan; if people saw Clinton's foreign policy as a basic change in direction from that of President George H. W. Bush; whether the federal government was spending too much, too little, or the right amount on national defense; and whether Clinton's proposed cuts in military and defense spending went too far, were about right, or didn't go far enough. These were not issues with which most people had intimate knowledge. And in all cases, there were no questions that measured how much people knew about these subjects. The question about the last issue was especially noteworthy because it essentially told respondents that Clinton was proposing cuts in defense spending and then immediately asked whether the cuts went too far or not. Clearly, we didn't want to know if the respondents had any inkling of what Clinton had specifically proposed—we just wanted their immediate, top-of-mind reaction to the information we were feeding them, so that we could report something we would proclaim "public opinion."

The problem was that we had chosen our sample of respondents using careful statistical procedures so that it would represent the larger population of Americans across the country, but once we began feeding our respondents information, they no longer represented that larger population. Some people in the larger population, of course, already knew that Clinton's economic plan included defense cuts, but many—perhaps even a majority—did not. Unless we could inform all Americans across the country about the defense cuts in exactly the same way we did in the survey, which was obviously impossible, the sample of respondents would no longer represent all Americans. Our claim, then, that we were measuring the general public's opinion was simply false.

At the end of April 1993, CNN and USA Today came up

with a poll to measure how President Clinton was doing after his first 100 days in office. We repeated the questions about Clinton's economic program that we had asked earlier in the year, but then followed up with a question about something that we were certain most people had not been following. "As you may know [we always introduced a question this way when we assumed that most people *didn't* know], President Clinton was forced to drop his economic stimulus package this week because of opposition from Republicans in the U.S. Senate." The economic stimulus package was separate from Clinton's overall economic plan, and only the most attentive news junkies would have known that—*and* the fact that the Republicans had killed it. But having just told respondents what the general public mostly did not know, we then asked a very biased question: "How do you feel about this—did Republicans do the *right thing* by stopping unnecessary government spending, or did they do the *wrong thing* by continuing the gridlock that prevents government from taking needed action on the economy?"

The question struck me as a disturbing approach to measuring what the public was thinking. Not only did we feed respondents information about something almost certainly only a small percentage knew, but then we offered tendentious reasons why the Republicans' action was either the right or wrong thing to do. Essentially, the uninformed respondents were judging between two assertions made by Gallup interviewers—that the Republicans stopped unnecessary spending, or that they continued gridlock. On either side, there could be serious objections to the phrasing of the two options provided in the questions. Democrats would hardly like the stimulus package to be characterized as "unnecessary" spending, and Republicans would be offended that opposing a bill would be called "gridlock." This question was clearly the media pollsters' attempt to shape respondents' opinions to fit their ongoing news story. The 52 percent to 41 percent result in favor of saying the Republicans did the "right thing" by killing the economic stimulus (with only 7 percent having no opinion) was a clear example of how we pollsters extract politically charged responses on even the most obscure topics.

At the time, I remember asking our two polling representatives from *USA Today* and CNN why they didn't seem to care about portraying the truth about public ignorance on most issues. The CNN representative (who has long since gone on to another position) took offense at such impolitic language and chastised me on the phone for my attitude. "It is not our business to tell the public what they don't know," he said. Initially, I was dismayed that Gallup would go along with such a position, but I soon realized that it wasn't just the Gallup Poll that downplayed public ignorance. If you take a look at all the other media polls, none systematically presents public opinion in the context of how much people know about an issue, how committed they are to their opinion, and how important that issue is to them. Instead we get a manufactured opinion based on a mythological public—measures that look like they represent what a rational, informed, and engaged citizenry might be thinking.

The Search for Meaning in Responses

The problem with manufactured opinion was recognized early on by the pioneer pollsters of the 1930s and 1940s. In 1942, Elmo Roper wrote in an essay for *Fortune* magazine titled "So the Blind Shall Not Lead" that even then, less than a decade since the advent of modern polling, "the emphasis in public opinion research has been largely misplaced. I believe its first duty is to explore the areas of public ignorance."[5] His views were reinforced by one of Gallup's severest critics at the time, Lindsay Rogers, who noted that "large segments of the electorate confess ignorance of many political questions" but such information was ignored when the pollsters announced the results of their polls.[6]

Another early public opinion scholar, Daniel Katz, also emphasized the importance of going beyond the superficial measures provided by polls. Katz wrote a chapter in a 1944 book titled *Gauging Public Opinion,* in which he argued that "to interpret poll results adequately it is necessary to know whether an expressed attitude represents a superficially held view which may be discarded the next moment or whether it reflects a cherished conviction which will change only under unusual pressure." In his view, it was crucial to measure the intensity of an opinion to determine, "for example, whether or not an individual with a given opinion holds that opinion strongly enough to take the trouble to go out and vote for it or fight for it."[7]

George Gallup responded to these criticisms by providing his own solution to the problem of non-opinion in a 1947 article in *Public Opinion Quarterly.*[8] He proposed a five-step method, a "quintamensional plan," for asking people about any public policy issue. The first step was to find out if respondents had even heard of the policy. For example, in November 1953, Gallup asked about the Taft-Hartley Act, which had received a great deal of attention over many months. He found that despite the news coverage, 60 percent of the respondents in a poll said they had not "followed" the discussion. Among the rest, 19 percent wanted to change the act, 11 percent to leave it as is, and 3 percent to repeal it. An additional 7 percent said they had followed the discussion but still had no opinion on what to do with the law (see fig. 4).

That kind of description simply doesn't appear in the current media accounts of public opinion. Today's media don't find it interesting to report that two-thirds of the people have no opinion about a major public policy issue, so the polls simply avoid measuring what the media don't want to report.

Gallup also proposed asking other questions about each policy issue, to include open-ended questions that would allow respondents to describe in their own words what they knew about the policy proposal and why they supported or opposed

FIGURE 4

What To Do With Taft-Hartley Act?

Gallup Poll, November, 1953

(in percent)

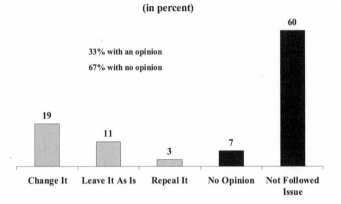

it. But that part of his proposal has never been systematically applied to policy issues. In several discussions I had with Alec Gallup over the years,[9] he said that the "quintamensional plan" devised by his father was never routinely used because it just wasn't practical for the news media. It required too many minutes of interviewing and too much analysis of the data once the interview was completed. In this case, "too much" meant the news media simply wanted a faster approach to measuring opinion. But a consequence of faster is superficiality.

In the 1980s, a highly renowned pollster and psychologist, Daniel Yankelovich, worked with *Time* magazine to design a simple battery of questions to determine whether responses to questions reflected public views that were firmly and thoughtfully held or views that were likely to change from one question to another.[10] Yankelovich suggested *Time* could use a marker, such as an asterisk, to indicate for each set of reported opinions whether the findings were stable or "mushy." The magazine editors embraced the idea, paid for the research, and shared the resulting index with several other organizations. Yankelovich called it a "volatility index," whereas *Time* preferred the more colloquial "mushiness index." In the end, *Time* abandoned the project and never used the new measure, preferring to remain with the prevailing superficial approach, which was easier and less costly.

Part of Yankelovich's concern was that the current method of conducting media polls undermines the confidence that people can place in polls. Different polls will inevitably produce different findings, because pollsters refuse to take into consideration people's level of knowledge or commitment to their views. Yankelovich was particularly concerned that media pollsters today do not examine the several stages that the public goes through as it confronts policy issues, from first being aware of an issue to eventually arriving at a "full deliberative judgment." Instead, he complained, media pollsters take a "snapshot" of public opinion as it is evolving and then provide no explanation as to the quality of that measured opinion.[11]

How Closely People Follow the News

Though it's fallen out of vogue for pollsters to ask respondents how much they know about an issue, some will ask respondents how closely they have paid attention to related news. The assumption is that the more attention people pay to an issue, the more they know about it. But as assumptions go, this is a poor one; self-reported news attention and knowledge are not the same thing. Moreover, we know that even when people are familiar enough with an issue to express an opinion, it doesn't mean they care whether their opinion prevails.

Still, asking people if they have heard of an issue is at least one step toward exploring beneath the surface of most reported opinion. When George Gallup polled on the Taft-Hartley Act, for example, he first asked if respondents had heard of the act. Only those people who said they had were asked the follow-up question. Not so most pollsters these days, including the SRI-owned Gallup Poll, which has adopted the common practice of asking *all* respondents to weigh in on a policy, even when they've already admitted they know little or nothing about it.

It's true that on many occasions, people who don't know anything about an issue respond similarly to those who do, usually because questions in the survey contain so much descriptive information that essentially all respondents are influenced by the same framing of the issue. On many other occasions, however, people who say they are paying attention to an issue express very different views from those who first learn about an issue from the interviewer. Often the views of the informed are lumped in with the views of the previously uninformed, a distortion of the true nature of public opinion on the issue.

That was the case with Gallup's polls on a French drug, RU-486, referred to by its critics as an "abortion pill" and by its supporters as the "morning-after pill." In April 2000, Gallup found a plurality of the public, 47 percent to 39 percent, opposed to making RU-486 available in the United States as a prescription drug (see fig. 5).[12] By the following October, when respondents were asked their views on "the recent decision by the Federal Drug Administration" to authorize the sale of RU-486 as a prescription drug, the tide had turned: the poll found that 50 percent were in favor, 44 percent opposed.[13] Two years later, Gallup's "in-depth review" of public attitudes on the general issue of abortion characterized public opinion on RU-486 as one of several areas that "sharply divide" the public. The review noted that "substantial disagreement also exists over . . . legalizing the French abortion pill known as RU-486," then reiterated that "Americans are closely divided about the matter."[14] What the report did not note was that people who had heard about RU-486 in the news *before* being asked about it by Gallup were substantially in favor of its being sold as a prescription drug, whereas people who heard of the drug for the first time in the Gallup interview were mostly opposed to its being sold.

FIGURE 5

Favor or Oppose RU-486 As a Prescription Drug?

(Gallup Poll, March 30-April 2, 2000)

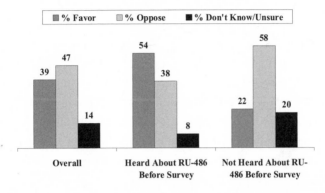

The specific question included in the April 2000 survey asked respondents whether they had "heard or read anything about RU-486, the so-called abortion pill?" It was probably that characterization of the drug that provoked immediate opposition among people who had never previously heard of it, since "abortion pill" hardly gives an adequate description of how or when the drug works. Perhaps some respondents thought it was designed to be taken weeks or months into a pregnancy. Gallup could have described RU-486 as "the pill women take shortly after sexual intercourse in order to avoid having a baby" or used other similarly less charged language. Or Gallup could have just ended the question after "RU-486," without giving any information at all. But Gallup chose to feed biased information to people who didn't know anything about the drug so that everyone in the sample could be asked the follow-up question.

How Gallup initially characterized the drug may not have made any difference if the follow-up question had been asked only of the 54 percent of people who said that they had heard or read something about the drug before being asked about it in the survey. But Gallup did ask everyone, including the 45 percent who said they had not heard or read *anything* about it: "Would you personally favor or oppose making RU-486—an abortion pill—available in the United States as a prescription drug?" The unknowing respondents had now been told twice that RU-486 was "an abortion pill," and nothing else. That group opposed making it a prescription drug by an overwhelming majority, 58 percent to 22 percent. Among those who knew about the drug *before* Gallup referred to it as "an abortion pill," there was a 16-point margin of support, 54 percent to 38 percent.

The following October, Gallup changed the question from whether people had heard or read anything about the drug (with a yes-no response), to asking how closely people were following the news about it, offering four possible responses: very closely, somewhat closely, not too closely, or not at all closely. The four response categories for following the news were then collapsed into two—very/somewhat closely, and not too/not at all closely—yielding about the same percentages who were attentive and not attentive in October as in April. In the later survey, 56 percent said they had followed the issue either very or somewhat closely, while 43 percent had not. The other wording was identical, with RU-486 still characterized as the "so-called abortion pill" in the first question, and "an abortion pill" in the second.

The October results among people who had heard of the drug before the interview were similar to those obtained in April—this time a 17-point margin in favor of the FDA decision to authorize its sale, 57 percent to 40 percent, hardly different from the 54 percent to 38 percent results of the previous spring. The biggest differences occurred among those who had not been following the news about the drug. This group was apparently very much influenced by the knowledge Gallup gave them that the FDA had authorized use of the drug, because the net opposition in the second survey was only 8 points (49 percent opposed, 41 percent in favor) whereas the previous negative margin was 36 points (see fig. 6).

FIGURE 6

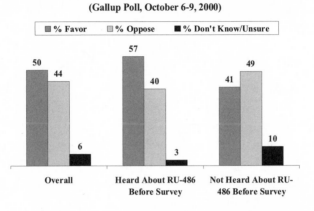

Favor or Oppose FDA Decision
On RU-486 To Be a Prescription Drug?

(Gallup Poll, October 6-9, 2000)

■ % Favor   □ % Oppose   ■ % Don't Know/Unsure

	Overall	Heard About RU-486 Before Survey	Not Heard About RU-486 Before Survey
% Favor	50	57	41
% Oppose	44	40	49
% Don't Know/Unsure	6	3	10

The Gallup "in-depth" report made no mention of the fact that among people who knew about RU-486, there was a substantial margin of support in the drug's favor. The *real* "sharp divide" in the public, not mentioned by that Gallup report, was between the half who knew something about the drug and the half who did not.

In my view, an accurate characterization of public opinion based on these Gallup surveys should have been that just over half of Americans had heard of RU-486, and that among this group, there was a clear majority in favor (more than a 15-point margin) of the FDA's allowing the sale of RU-486 as a prescription drug. Gallup didn't measure intensity, so we can't conclude that even among those with an opinion, most wanted their views to prevail—only that at least a majority of those who knew about the drug were willing for the authorization to occur. Also, a little less than half of Americans hadn't heard of the drug, so we can't say what their opinions were. We do know that knowledge and ignorance of RU-486 were shared about equally among people who classified themselves as pro-choice and pro-life, based on an analysis of the April poll data. Thus, the "informed" or "attentive" public was not disproportionately preordained toward either support or opposition.

Gallup's approach to polling on RU-486 was inadvisable for at least three reasons. The first is that feeding respondents any information about a complex and controversial issue almost necessarily involves using biased language. To call RU-486 an "abortion pill" would be like calling the female contraceptive IUD an "abortion device" or characterizing the discarding of embryos as "killing" human beings. That approach certainly satisfies people at one end of the political spectrum, but there are less didactic and still accurate ways to describe RU-486, which could elicit different responses. Gallup should have avoided any bias by simply asking if people had heard of RU-486 and stopping there.

The second inadvisable move that Gallup made was describing RU-486 at all. By feeding respondents any description of the drug, Gallup contaminated the sample so that the respondents no longer represented Americans across the country—because the rest of the country had not been given the same information about RU-486. An argument often heard in support of giving respondents selected facts about certain issues is that the tactic allows pollsters to measure what the public *would* think if it had that information. But that argument is both inaccurate and disingenuous. It's inaccurate because it will never be the case that all Americans will be informed about some issue in the same way poll respondents are. Not all Americans will be told, for example, that RU-486 is an abortion pill with no other information provided. And the argument is disingenuous because the poll results are not reported as what the public *would* think if it were informed, but rather as what the public *does* think. The Gallup in-depth report made no mention of the results being hypothetical, but rather claimed that the public was, at that time, "sharply divided" on the issue of RU-486.

The final problem with Gallup's polling on RU-486 is that the results were wrong. The public was not sharply divided on RU-486. In fact, the public was largely ignorant of the drug, but among those who had heard of it, there was substantial support for allowing it to be sold as a prescription. That's the truth of the matter. And you won't find it in the Gallup report.[15]

Force-Feeding Respondents

Pollsters rarely ask people about their attentiveness to the news before feeding them information, the concern being that the poll could undermine its own credibility when respondents who admit they know little or nothing about an issue are asked about it anyway. Instead, pollsters are more likely to follow the example of a 2005 ABC News/*Washington Post* Poll in which interviewers told respondents, "The Senate has confirmed thirty-five federal appeals court judges nominated by Bush, while Senate Democrats have blocked ten others," then immediately asked, "Do you think the Senate Democrats are right or wrong to block those nominations?"[16] This is a typical forced-choice format question, offering no explicit "don't know" response, and pressuring respondents to give an answer. Yet 13 percent were brave enough to ignore the forced choices and say they didn't know if the Democrats were right or wrong. And although pollsters wanted respondents to say that either *all* the blocked nominations were wrong or *all* were right, 3 percent of respondents volunteered the opinion that the Democrats were right to block some and wrong to block others. The rest of the respondents bought into the very narrow framework presented by the poll, with 48 percent saying the Democrats were right to block all ten nominations and 36 percent saying the Democrats were wrong all ten times.

The problems with the ABC News/*Washington Post* Poll should be obvious to anyone who thinks carefully about the question. It may tap into partisan feelings—with mostly Democrats saying the Democrats were right and mostly Republicans saying the Democrats were wrong—but the question hardly taps into a public judgment about the specific action that is mentioned. We have no idea how many people were aware that the Democrats had blocked *any* judges, much less what respondents knew about each of the blocked nominations and whether there were good grounds for the Democrats' actions.

The tactic of providing information and then immediately asking respondents to make a judgment based on what they've been told is used by most media polls, including the CBS News/*New York Times* Poll. In March 2007, its interviewers told respondents, "As you may know, members of the Bush administration have accused Iran of supporting Iraqi insurgents by supplying them with weapons to use against American forces."[17] That could well have been news to a lot of Americans, possibly even a majority. The poll was careful not to find out. Interviewers quickly asked, "When members of the Bush administration talk about Iran's involvement in Iraq, do you think they are telling the entire truth, mostly telling the truth but hiding something, or are they mostly lying?" Amazingly, only 6 percent said they didn't know. Either the public was unusually attentive on that issue, or a whole lot of people simply expressed their gut reaction about the Bush administration *in general*—not necessarily about the Bush administration's accusations concerning Iran. Yet the two news outlets could report that 80 percent of Americans were skeptical about the Bush administration's accusations *regarding Iran,* with 24 percent saying the members of the Bush administration were "mostly lying," and 56 percent saying the Bush officials were "hiding something."

One of the more elaborate attempts to create public opinion when there may not have been any came during a 2005 *Los Angeles Times* poll.[18] Respondents who had the misfortune of picking up their phones that day heard the following:

As you may know, another issue that is on Bush's agenda is to reform medical liability awards. The President would like to put a $250,000 cap on jury awards for pain and suffering. The Bush Administration contends that excessive damage awards have become a burden for businesses and a drag on the nation's economy. They argue that the cost of frivolous lawsuits make it prohibitively expensive for small businesses to stay in business or for doctors to practice medicine. Opponents say the White House is exaggerating the extent of the problem of excessive damage awards, and say that caps on damages ultimately do not reduce premiums for doctors. They acknowledge the high cost of malpractice insurance, but blame it on lax regulation of the insurance industry. Do you approve or disapprove of capping damages awarded by juries to $250,000 for pain and suffering?

It's hard to imagine that many respondents actually absorbed the details of this long-winded exposition on liability awards, so it may be a surprise that a measly 8 percent admitted that they were unsure how to answer the question. The other 92 percent gave a response, one might guess, solely to prevent the interviewer from rereading the question. From the media's point of view, however, the poll worked just fine. Fifty percent approved of the Bush proposal, 42 percent disapproved. It certainly sounded newsworthy, and who could prove that it wasn't?

I WISH I COULD SAY that the examples cited here are isolated. Unfortunately, they are part of a routine process by which all media pollsters create a public opinion that serves the news media but does not serve the public or its elected representatives. Oversimplifying complex issues, using the forced-choice format, avoiding questions that might reveal how little people know or care about issues, and feeding respondents information are all part of the manufacturing process. As Daniel Yan-kelovich laments, "Sad to say, the media who sponsor opinion polls on policy issues have little or no stake in the quality of the poll findings they report."[19] This sad state of news media cover-age is a far cry from what George Gallup and the *Washington Post* envisioned almost three-quarters of a century ago when they announced with great fanfare the new journalistic "beat" of public opinion.

CHAPTER THREE

Telling Americans What They Think

On Sunday, October 20, 1935, an unusual sighting occurred over Washington, D.C.: a blimp pulling a long streamer that heralded a new era in American journalism with the words "America Speaks!" The blimp had been hired by the *Washington Post* editor Eugene Meyer to mark the first installment of a weekly column by George Gallup of the American Institute of Public Opinion. What the public thought about issues would, for the first time in the history of American journalism, be included as an integral part of news reporting. And Meyer wanted the whole world, and certainly his own city, to know about it. A few years later, Meyer would express his continued enthusiasm for this revolution in modern journalism, writing, "I have felt from the beginning that the publication of Dr. Gallup's reporting of essential facts . . . has been a most useful and constructive contribution to the successful operation of the democratic system."[1] Such a contribution was certainly the ambitious young pollster's intent, but as to the actual effects of polls on democracy, it's been a source of contention since America began speaking to George Gallup.

BY THE TIME Gallup launched his weekly reports of public opinion, straw polls had long been a part of the journalistic enterprise. They usually were part of efforts by the press to get an early read during election season on how people might vote. The term "straw poll" is derived from the idea that someone will take a straw and throw it into the air to see which way the wind is blowing—in this context, to gauge the political winds.[2] These straw polls were mostly informal, and, although they provided interesting news stories, they weren't treated as serious predictions of election outcomes. We see similar gimmicks today, when news stations and newspapers invite viewers and readers to submit their opinions on some issue, but hardly anyone thinks such results reflect the general population.

A few newspapers in the early part of the twentieth century saw the polls less as a publicity ploy than as a serious method for gaining insight into the voters' minds. They used sampling techniques that were relatively rigorous in specifying which voters to interview to ensure that poll participants would more closely represent the larger voting population. The *Cincinnati Enquirer,* for example, conducted six statewide straw polls on the presidential contest between 1908 and 1928. On average the results were accurate to within 2 percentage points of the final results. The *Chicago Journal* conducted twelve straw polls in the city between 1905 and 1928, and their accuracy rate improved considerably over time. Their first six straw polls differed from the final results by an average of 6 percentage points, whereas the last six differed by an average of only 2 points.[3]

One media outlet that didn't attempt to use rigorous sampling methods but nevertheless helped popularize the use of straw polls was the *Literary Digest,* a weekly general-interest magazine similar in format to today's *Time* and *Newsweek.*[4] The *Digest* flirted with conducting a straw poll in 1916, when it mailed questionnaire-style "ballots" to subscribers in five states asking them to indicate their own presidential preferences and to report on what the political sentiment was in their communities. The *Digest's* editors were so pleased with the venture that four years later they sent ballots to more than 11 million people. Because the straw poll was conducted before the parties had decided on presidential nominees, however, the results could not be used to predict the general election.

For the next three presidential elections, the *Digest* mailed its ballots after the party conventions. The timing would allow the magazine to predict the final winner. Perhaps even more important, each week, as more ballots were returned, the update provided another exciting news story–each loudly trumpeted by the magazine: "Ballots, ballots, ballots—fresh from the printing-press, done up in great packages, they're beginning to pour in to *The Literary Digest's* presidential poll headquarters, some days a million and some a million-and-a-half."[5]

In each of those election years, the *Digest* correctly predicted the winner—Calvin Coolidge over John Davis and Robert LaFollette (the Progressive Party candidate) in 1924, Herbert Hoover over Al Smith in 1928, and Franklin Delano Roosevelt over Herbert Hoover in 1932. The last prediction was particularly noteworthy. Not only did the magazine predict the percentage of the vote favoring Roosevelt (59.14) within three-quarters of a percentage point of the actual vote (59.85 percent), it correctly predicted the presidential winner in 43 of the 48 states, with an average error of just 3 percentage points. Two of the five incorrectly predicted states actually supported Hoover, and the other three supported Roosevelt, tending to cancel the overall error. The *Digest's* final prediction showed Roosevelt winning 41 states with 474 electoral votes, whereas he wound up winning 42 states with 472 electoral votes.[6]

By any standard now or then, this was a truly impressive performance. Newspapers across the country referred to the poll's "uncanny" accuracy, and the *Digest's* editors, unable to contain their pride, published several newspaper testimonials. "We want to display some of the bouquets that are being thrown at the poll from all over the country," they wrote. "All we can say in answer to the loud applause is this: 'When better polls are built, the *Digest* will build them.'"[7]

Unrecognized by the editors were two persistent and related problems that would ultimately lead to the *Digest*'s demise. Its samples of voters were biased in favor of upper income people, and that same economic tier was more likely to answer mail ballots. The magazine had what statisticians today call a sampling problem as well as a nonresponse problem, both of which biased their results in favor of Republicans. The sampling problem was caused by the fact that the ballots were sent primarily to people who had telephones and automobiles, because it was easy to obtain addresses from automobile registrations and from telephone directories—what researchers of the day referred to as the "tel-auto" lists. The nonresponse problem was caused by the fact that people with lower income and a lower level of education were less interested in filling out the ballots, which included invitations to subscribe or resubscribe to the *Digest*.[8] These solicitations were apparently quite successful. After one mailing, the *Digest* informed its advertisers, "Almost overnight, we have advanced circulation tremendously."[9] As one might easily surmise, the success was particularly noticeable among higher income voters.

Given their experience with the presidential polls, especially the 1932 poll, the editors had no reason to doubt their methodology. They were convinced that their polling sample was a good representation of the American public. The *Topeka Capital,* one of the newspapers that sent congratulations to the *Digest* for its 1932 poll, was explicit: "What [the poll] demonstrates is that telephone numbers and automobile numbers are representative of the United States, not only politically but generally.... *Telephone numbers and automobile tags represent the United States!*"[10]

It was the midst of the Great Depression, and a lot of people who couldn't afford to own cars and telephones were automatically excluded from the *Digest* poll. But even before that, Claude Robinson, a Columbia University scholar who later worked with George Gallup, noted that the "tel-auto" list used by the *Digest* was likely to cause problems. Republicans were overrepresented in every state in the 1928 straw poll, and in all but seven states in the 1924 poll—which also had LaFollette coming in second, rather than his poor third in the real election.[11] This overrepresentation of Republicans appeared to be directly related to the economic bias in the samples and to the nonresponse of lower income voters. But because Republican candidates won in the 1924 and 1928 elections, the bias didn't affect the *Digest* polls when it came to predicting the winner, though it did raise red flags by projecting winning percentages that were considerably higher than the actual results.

In 1932, in the aftermath of the stock market crash and the effects of the Depression, people in the higher economic strata were as dissatisfied with President Hoover as poorer people were, so voting preferences in the higher and lower economic strata were similar. In a rare crossover, upper income Americans voted Democratic, and Roosevelt won in the landslide that the *Digest* accurately predicted. Once again, the economic bias in the *Digest*'s sample of Americans went undetected. But in 1936, the chickens would come home to roost.

George Gallup's genius lay in recognizing the flaws of the *Digest*'s polling operation and in applying updated market research sampling methods to cut down on the expense of national sampling. Whereas the *Digest* sent out millions of ballots, Gallup polled only a few thousand people. Initially, he experimented with sending out mail ballots, but he quickly recognized the nonresponse problem and abandoned that effort. Instead, he hired interviewers, mostly people who lived in the geographical areas he wanted surveyed, but some who would drive from state to state. He used a strict system of quota sampling, which was the "scientific" part of the poll, to ensure that people in all parts of the country and at all economic levels would be included according to their proportions in the national census. This approach eliminated the sampling problem inherent in the *Digest*'s "tel-auto" samples. In each geographical area selected by Gallup, interviewers had to find people who fit the various categories by age, income, and gender, which minimized the problem of nonresponse bias. Though direct refusals were quite low, if one voter declined to participate, the interviewers would have to find another who fit the needed demographic profile.

After four years of Roosevelt's "New Deal" economic policies, the *Digest*'s tel-auto list of people in the upper economic strata were ready for the return of a Republican in the White House. And, sure enough, the *Digest*'s poll predicted that Alf Landon would beat Roosevelt 57 percent to 42 percent. The upstart Gallup, by contrast, controversially forecasted a Roosevelt victory vote of 54 percent to 46 percent. Roosevelt actually won with 61 percent of the vote—7 percentage points more than Gallup had predicted, but 19 points more than the *Digest*'s final results. Though Gallup was upset over the 7-point margin, he had proven that his new "scientific" polling approach worked, and he had helped usher in a new era of public opinion polling.

GALLUP WAS NOT the only scientific pollster to weigh in that election year. Two other market researchers, Archibald Crossley and Elmo Roper, had already begun conducting national polls before Gallup founded his institute. And they, too, predicted Roosevelt's reelection. But in the aftermath of the 1936 election, it was Gallup who became the great evangelist on behalf of polls, not just to predict election outcomes, but to give voice to the people. That had been his intention all along, as reflected in the title of his column, "America Speaks!" He made much of the writings of British scholar James Bryce,[12] who called for the dominant role of public opinion in modern representative governments. Translating public opinion into policy,

Bryce argued, required frequent input from the people, but "the machinery for weighing or measuring the popular will from week to week or month to month is not likely to be invented." A little more than a half century later, Gallup announced that the machinery had, in fact, been invented:

> The development of a careful sampling technique has virtually overcome the obstacles of time and expense which caused Bryce to doubt the possibility of continuous nation-wide referendums. By collecting the opinions of a representative sample of voters, they have made possible that week-to-week audit of public opinion, which Bryce himself called the "logical resource."[13]

Gallup was not the first to examine the public's views on political and social issues. In 1907, the *Chicago Journal* conducted a straw poll on the issue of a city traction ordinance, and the *Literary Digest* over the years had cranked up its polling machinery to measure people's views on the soldier's bonus (1922), the Mellon Tax Plan (1924), and Prohibition (1922, 1930, and 1932).[14] But the principal focus of the early straw polls was on elections. With the advent of the scientific polls, the emphasis shifted to a much wider sampling of the public's views and habits.

The very first question Gallup highlighted in his new weekly column was whether "expenditures by the Government for relief and recovery are too little, too great, or about right."[15] Though the country was still in the midst of the Great Depression, 60 percent of Gallup's respondents said the government was spending too much, 31 percent said about right, and 9 percent said too little. He compared those results with those he had obtained the previous year, while experimenting with his new polling method, to show a decline in support for Roosevelt's New Deal policies.

In the first several years, Gallup polled on a number of other political topics: minimum wage, child labor, performance of various agencies of the New Deal, old age insurance, labor unions, states' rights, federal spending, inflation, mercy killing, universal fingerprinting, lynching, divorce, Prohibition, capital punishment, the Supreme Court, birth control, and whether the country should become involved or remain neutral in the war in Europe. Gallup also asked some purely cultural questions about the use of alcohol, women working in business when their husbands could afford to support them, what schools should teach about government, the ideal family size, favorite sport to watch, the use of automobiles, and the acceptability of men wearing topless bathing suits. The *Fortune Quarterly Survey* conducted by Roper included some of these and other topics, but it was Gallup's weekly reports that provided by far the more frequent and extensive coverage of the political and cultural landscape of the country.[16]

With his journalism background, Gallup was particularly sensitive to what he saw as the needs of the news media, ensuring that many of the topics he covered could be integrated into the news stories of the day. And very quickly, even before he demonstrated the accuracy of his polls in the 1936 presidential election, his results began having a major influence in Washington, D.C.

At the time Gallup launched his weekly column, poverty among the elderly was a major social problem, and the grassroots movement for the Townsend Plan was at its peak.[17] First suggested by Dr. Francis Townsend in a letter to a Long Beach newspaper in early 1933, it proposed that the federal government give every retired couple $200 per month providing they were at least sixty years of age and would spend the money within thirty days, which would help stimulate the economy. Favorable response was swift and massive, spawning local organizations throughout the country that drew in more than two million members. The movement was so powerful it helped spur Roosevelt to propose his own old-age pension plan, which became the Social Security Act, passed in 1935. But the

Townsendites were not satisfied and continued to pressure Congress for passage of the more generous and expensive Townsend Plan. As a result, several bills were introduced into Congress in 1935 and 1936 that would have enacted into law most of the plan's features.

It was in this political environment in December 1935 that Gallup asked respondents five questions on the matter. The first was whether respondents were in favor of government old-age pensions for needy persons. A resounding 89 percent said they were. These respondents were then asked three follow-up questions. How much should be paid monthly to each single person? The average: $40 per month. How much should be paid monthly to a married couple? The average: $60 (average monthly household income at the time was $100). Finally, what age should a person be to qualify for an old age pension? The average: 60 years. Then all respondents were asked if they favored the Townsend Plan—"that is, paying $200 a month to each aged husband and wife?" Just 3.8 percent said yes, 96.2 percent no. According to Claude Robinson, writing in 1937, "After publication of these figures, Townsend's influence over Congress suffered a sharp decline, and within a month a resolution had been voted to investigate his movement."[18]

Another of Gallup's early influential polls was on the subject of venereal disease, which at the time was estimated to afflict about one in ten adult Americans. Although there had been successful public health campaigns against such diseases as diphtheria and tuberculosis, social taboos made it difficult for government officials to get widespread publicity about the symptoms and treatment of gonorrhea and syphilis. Newspapers and radio stations simply would not cover stories about the causes and cures of these venereal diseases, even when promulgated by government health authorities. "Fear of offending the public through discussions of venereal disease," complained the U.S. surgeon general, "is first and foremost among American handicaps in progress against syphilis."[19] As Gallup would later acknowledge, it was "with some trepidation" that he decided to include a question on the subject in a December 1936 poll, which asked whether respondents would be in "favor of a government bureau that would distribute information concerning venereal diseases?" Much to his surprise, 88 percent said yes. A month later, he asked whether Congress should appropriate $25 million to help control venereal disease. Another surprise: more than 90 percent said yes. The notion that the public would be offended by public health efforts to control the disease took another hit in Gallup's July 1937 survey, when 87 percent of respondents said yes to the question, "In strict confidence and at no expense to you, would you like to be given, by your own physician, a blood test for syphilis?"[20] Gallup later wrote, "It is gratifying to observe that during the past year, discussions of the social disease have been broadcast from our principal radio stations and carried in the columns of scores of newspapers."[21]

THOUGH GALLUP WAS enthusiastic about his newly developed ability to "monitor the pulse of democracy," others were quite critical. Some scholars denounced the notion that public opinion, as measured by polls, was simply "an aggregation of equally weighted individual opinions." To the contrary, they argued, public opinion had meaning only in a societal context, where it is expressed through groups and institutions.[22] Summing up the number of people in support or opposition to a policy had no relevant meaning in the way government operates, where conflicting preferences have to be traded off against available resources. Opponents didn't take issue with Gallup's results that dealt with people's personal lives, like the number of people who were willing to have a test for syphilis. What critics objected to was the kind of poll results that showed Americans supporting a $25 million allocation to fight venereal disease, since no mention was made of other programs that might also receive such an allocation or of the way the program would be funded. The fact that so many Americans supported the proposal meant *something*—at the very least, a general consensus that venereal disease was a problem that should be addressed, and that, contrary to popular belief, there was no social taboo against discussing it publicly. But opponents of Gallup's approach to public opinion argued that such policy results couldn't be taken as a concrete demand by the public. Congress shouldn't immediately start writing a check for $25 million.

Other scholars dismissed polls because of their inherent limitations, primarily that they can pose only the simplest of questions. A prime example would be Gallup's very first question, whether the government was spending too much, too little, or the right amount on relief and recovery. The results showed a general public feeling that too much was being spent, without any guidance as to what specifically in the budget, if anything, should be cut. And that's true of most of Gallup's questions of the day, such as one he asked in September 1935: "In order to declare war, should Congress be required to obtain the approval of the people by means of a national vote?"[23] Three-quarters said yes. Of course that's not what our Constitution requires, nor obviously is it what happened after the Japanese attacked Pearl Harbor. Another question in the same survey asked simply, "If one foreign nation insists upon attacking another, should the United States join with other nations to compel it to stop?"[24] The question was so vague, with the answer clearly dependent on so many unknown factors, that critics hardly knew what to make of the response—71 percent of respondents said no, the rest answered yes. The effort to plumb the public will on complex issues by asking singular and oversimplified questions was at the heart of the arguments against Gallup's "sampling referendum." As one critic noted, "Instead of feeling the pulse of democracy, Dr. Gallup listens to its baby talk."[25]

President Dewey

The biggest setback to the burgeoning polling industry was the pollsters' failure in 1948, when all confidently predicted that Republican Thomas A. Dewey would defeat incumbent Democratic President Harry S. Truman. It's no exaggeration to say that nearly the entire country expected a Dewey victory. In part, these expectations were set up by the 1946 congressional midterm elections, when Republicans swept the Democrats out of office in both the House and Senate, regaining majority control of both houses for the first time since before the Depression. The solid defeat was largely attributed to Truman's poor performance in office, and it was widely expected that the 1948 election would see the completion of the Democratic Party's rout. When the three scientific pollsters all showed Dewey with a double-digit lead in the summer of 1948, any lingering doubts about a Republican victory that fall vanished.

Warning signs were there, however. Both the Crossley and Gallup polls showed significant movement in the next few months, with Gallup reporting a Dewey lead of 12 points in mid-July that was down to 5 points in mid-October, his last polling period. Crossley, too, showed Dewey with only a 5-point lead in his last poll, but neither pollster expected Truman's momentum to carry him to victory. Such rapid changes in voter preferences had never happened in the three previous presidential elections they had polled. Those elections, of course, were all dominated by Franklin Roosevelt, and public opinion about him was certainly firmer than the public's shifting sense of these two less well known candidates—as the pollsters were soon to discover. Truman won with 49.6 percent of the vote to Dewey's 45.1 percent.

After Truman's reelection, the most disastrous day in polling history, there was much gnashing of teeth and second-guessing about the causes of the pollsters' failure. Yet the explanation was quite simple: the pollsters had quit polling too early. Postelection surveys by both Gallup and Roper showed about one in seven voters making up their minds in the last two weeks of the campaign, and Truman winning three-quarters of that group. Those results support the conclusion that had the polls been conducted later, they would have tracked the final surge of support for Truman. After seven decades of polling data attesting time and time again to the mercurial nature of voter preference, no pollster today would even consider predicting a presidential winner based on polls conducted two weeks or longer before Election Day.

The postelection polls by Gallup and Roper, however, hit on another problem, one that is still ongoing—misgauging voter indecision. If so many voters were undecided in the last two weeks of the campaign, why didn't the pollsters pick up on that when they asked the voters which candidate they would support? In Gallup's report of his last preelection poll, October 15 through 25, he had allocated all of the undecided voters to one candidate or another, a decision that he later regretted. That was the modus operandi not only of Gallup but of the other pollsters of the day—they eliminated the undecided percentages in their last preelection poll by allocating those votes so that their final predictions would reflect what they expected the final vote count to be. As Crossley later explained, "We were told on all sides that the worst sin of poll reporting was hedging."[26]

Like his colleagues, Gallup assumed that those who were still undecided would probably cast their ballots proportional to what other voters had done. Since he didn't mention undecided voters in his October report, it's unclear how many he actually found. However, one month earlier Gallup had reported that 8 percent of the public was still undecided. It's a good bet that if Gallup found 8 percent of voters undecided in September, that number was probably close to the same a month later, if not lower. How, then, could Gallup's postelection survey show 14 percent undecided in the last two weeks? The problem was, and remains, that pollsters ask the wrong questions.

From the start of his polling enterprise, Gallup pressured respondents to say whom they would vote for "if the election were held today," a question that masks the true number of people who haven't made up their minds. To get an accurate measure of how many voters remained undecided in September and October, he should have first asked respondents whether they had even made a decision on which candidate they would support on *Election Day*. Even after the devastating Dewey miscall, Gallup never modified his wording to get a better measure of the undecided vote. Today pollsters still use Gallup's flawed horserace question.

Proliferation of Polls

For thirty years, Gallup was the most prominent and prolific source of public opinion information in the country. In 1956, Louis Harris, a young analyst who had worked for Elmo Roper for close to a decade, had a falling out with Roper and founded his own polling company. He became the most visible of a new breed of pollster, one who worked primarily for political campaigns. For the next seven years he worked for more than 240 candidates, most of them Democrats, including John Kennedy in the 1960 presidential contest. "I elected one president, one prime minister, about 28 governors, and maybe close to 60 U.S. Senators," he later boasted.[27] He also worked for the news media, helping first CBS and then ABC on its election night polling. In 1963, he gave up working for political candidates altogether to conduct polls solely for the media and for private clients, excluding political candidates running for office. From then until the advent of media-owned polls starting in the mid-1970s, he and Gallup were on a par as the two biggest promulgators of U.S. public opinion.

Harris's polling techniques, however, contrasted sharply with those pioneered and popularized by Gallup. While Gallup insisted on simple questions that could be understood by respondents, Harris often used what he called "projective" questions: he would give respondents complex and even biased information and then ask their reaction. Sometimes he would give both positive and negative information, and then see where the respondents ended up in their views. Also, unlike Gallup, Harris was often interested in using his polls as a platform for action, and his partisanship was never far from the surface.

In 1979, while Harris was polling for ABC News, Senator Ted Kennedy announced that he would challenge incumbent president Jimmy Carter in the Democratic Party primaries. This was great news to Harris, who had fond memories of his work with John Kennedy two decades earlier. Although Harris continued to poll for ABC News, he announced to his company's researchers, "I'm going to make the next president."[28] In the months that followed, Harris used projective questions and selective reporting to bias his polling reports in Kennedy's favor, and he followed a pattern of reporting good news about the Massachusetts senator while delaying, or even omitting, any favorable polls about President Carter.

For close to three decades, Louis Harris and Associates was one of the giants of polling, but Harris's legacy does not come anywhere near that of George Gallup's. His inability to separate his partisan biases from his public policy polling undermined his credibility. Harris sold his company in 1969, but he continued to run it until January 1992, when he resigned to start a new company, L.H. Research. He retired soon after that. His original company was bought by Gordon Black, and today it is called Harris Interactive and operates as a market research company that conducts both telephone and Internet polls for private clients.

DESPITE THE REGULAR USE of Gallup and Harris election polls by many news organizations throughout the 1960s and 1970s, the journalistic culture did not value public opinion data when it came to policy matters. Since the role of the general public in American democracy is not to make policy decisions but to elect representatives to do it for them, reporters tended to think of polls as most useful when they reported on how people might vote or on what might affect their vote. For the most part, journalists dismissed the notion that the average citizen would have much to say about arcane policy matters. At the end of the 1970s and into the 1980s, journalists' estimation of polls changed because of technological advances that made polling more feasible for news organizations. Prior to this period, it had been too expensive to hire teams of interviewers across the country to conduct in-person interviews at people's homes. But with the expansion of telephones into most Americans' homes, and a concomitant increase in the capacity and affordability of computers to process collected data, the costs were now manageable. In 1975, the *New York Times* and CBS News presented the first joint media poll. Interviews were conducted in the evening on telephones that were used by reporters and administrators during the day, with data analysis performed on newsroom computers that had become an integral part of the news process. Other news organizations soon followed suit, spurred on by the desire to control their own public opinion data, rather than have it selectively fed to them by the government and by political candidates, who were more and more frequently hiring pollsters. Little by little, journalists accepted the idea that they would cover public opinion as a news beat, much as they covered the White House, Congress, city hall, and other decision-making institutions.[29] By the mid-1980s, many national news organizations had either developed their own polls or were regularly commissioning polls for their exclusive use. From CBS and the *New York Times,* to the *Washington Post,* ABC News, NBC News, the *Wall Street Journal, Time, Newsweek, USA Today,* the Associated Press, CNN, and the *Los Angeles Times,* the public opinion beat had come into its own.

Questionable Ethics

The news media's decision to control its own polls was dogged by controversy. One of the most important objections came down to a simple point: when the media conduct their own polls, they are no longer reporting the news, but making it. According to Nicholas Von Hoffman, a veteran journalist and a columnist for the *New York Observer*, the situation was bad enough when papers subscribed to the Gallup Poll. The problem, he argued, was that polls weren't "news" in the regular sense of the word. Usually, something happens, and the press reports it. That something is news. In this case, with polls being created expressly for the press, their results met Von Hoffman's definition of a "pseudo-event": "a happening which is arranged, contrived, or orchestrated for the purpose of gaining publicity." He reluctantly acknowledged that reporters might be able to make the argument that this sort of "checkbook journalism" (paying Gallup for poll stories) could be considered akin to buying the right to cover a story, in the same sense that the media will buy the right to cover a boxing match. It was a weak argument, in his view, but at the edges it had some credibility. But when the news media conduct and commission their own polls, they have crossed the line and are now, in his words, "making their own news and flacking it as though it were an event they were reporting on over which they had no control, like an earthquake or a traffic accident. The ethics of the practice are by journalism's own canons indefensible. No reputable newspaper, no television network permits its correspondents to pay money to stage a news event. Anybody doing such a thing would be fired forthwith, but [news] corporations can routinely do what is unethical for their employees [to do]."[30]

Von Hoffman's argument is particularly cogent, given that the news organizations with their own polls tend to cover only their own polls, and not the poll results from other organiza-

tions. If an event is newsworthy, presumably all the news organizations would want to cover it. But that doesn't happen
with polls.

Of course, the sponsoring news organization has a vested
interest in covering its own poll and not any others, given the
time and expense of conducting surveys. Occasionally, a news
organization will mention other polls, sometimes for support,
and other times because a controversy has arisen over conflicting results. But for the most part, when any of the networks an-
nounces its latest presidential approval rating, for example, it
doesn't put that rating into the context of what other polls are
showing. And by the same token, other news organizations will
ignore the latest results from competitors if they already have
their own polling operations. Such was the case with the January 18, 2008, ABC poll report, headlined "Bush hits lowest approval rating yet in ABC poll."[31] Showing a 32 percent approval
rating, the article did not mention the many other media polls
when Bush's rating was lower. According to pollster.com, there
were more than fifty *previous* poll readings all lower than the
ABC figure, and all before the end of 2007. That included four-
teen lower readings from the CBS/*New York Times* poll, ten
from the *Newsweek* poll, and six from Pew.[32] The article went
on to acknowledge that the new approval rating was not significantly different from the ratings in the network's previous nine
polls. The big news was that this was "Bush's first rating below
the one-third mark" *in an ABC poll,* as though that milestone
was somehow a newsworthy item. Needless to say, no other
news organization felt compelled to report this piece of news.
Similarly, when *USA Today* announced on July 9, 2007, that a
USA Today/Gallup poll found Bush's job approval at 29 percent,
his lowest ever, that reporter also didn't see fit to mention that
eleven previous poll readings from other organizations had already reported ratings that low or even lower.[33] When a news
organization creates information that only it finds worthwhile to

report, criticisms such as those leveled by Von Hoffman seem right on the money.

MORE THAN SEVEN DECADES after Eugene Meyer's blimp announced the advent of George Gallup's column and a new era in American journalism, most people would agree with CBS News Poll director Kathleen Frankovic, who wrote, "Polls are not only part of the news today, they are news. They not only sample public opinion, they define it."[34] Most of the scholarly objections to "public opinion" as defined by polls have largely been overridden, at least in the popular use of the term. In most people's minds, certainly in the mind of media pollsters, public opinion is what the pollsters can measure. Ethical objections to the news media's polling operations for producing pseudo-events and making their own news have also been overridden, not so much by rational discourse as by widespread practice. Logic or reasoning inevitably gives way to power. The news media find polls very useful, and there is little chance that any argument which might undermine them will prevail.

Still, there is a crisis in public policy polling today, a silent crisis that no one wants to talk about it. The problem lies not in the declining response rates and increasing difficulty in obtaining representative samples, though these are issues the polling industry has to address. The crisis lies, rather, in the refusal of media polls to tell the truth about those surveyed and about the larger electorate. Rather than tell us the "essential facts" about the public, as Meyer envisioned, they feed us a fairy-tale picture of a completely rational, all-knowing, and fully engaged citizenry. They studiously avoid reporting on widespread public apathy, indecision, and ignorance. The net result is conflicting poll results and a distortion of public opinion that challenges the credibility of the whole polling enterprise. Nowhere is this more often the case than in election polling.

CHAPTER FOUR

Inscrutable Elections

Presidential elections have long been high-stakes proving grounds for pollsters. Ever since George Gallup used his 1936 results to demonstrate that his polling was superior to the straw-poll methodology of the *Literary Digest*, the press has paid close attention to the various polls' final election predictions. The assumption has always been that if polls can accurately predict elections, then their numbers during the campaign and in nonelection periods will be valid as well. Usually, most of the major media polls do predict the results of a presidential election within a small margin of error. And every quadrennium, the National Council of Public Polls issues a self-congratulatory news release about how well its members (the major media polls) have performed in the presidential election cycle. What that release doesn't mention, and what the press tends to overlook, is that the polls do an atrocious job during the campaign, when polling results frequently conflict with one another, and pollsters deliberately suppress important information about the voters. The net result is that media polls often present a highly misleading if not outright false picture of how the candidates are faring and what voters are thinking.

———

MONTHS, AND ESPECIALLY YEARS, before a presidential election, polls about hypothetical match-ups between potential candidates have no predictive value for the general election, as pollsters will readily admit. What most pollsters won't admit is that such polls also offer virtually no insight into how the campaign will unfold. Instead, pollsters blithely ask respondents who they would vote for "if the election were held today" and then report the results as though they provide real insights into the pending campaign.

Such was the case in December 2006, shortly after the midterm elections, when two news organizations weighed in with what would happen in the next national election, almost two years away. A *Newsweek* poll discovered that if Hillary Clinton, the presumed favorite among Democratic candidates, were to be pitted against John McCain, the presumed favorite among Republicans, Clinton would win by a 7-point margin, 50 percent to 43 percent, with just 7 percent undecided.[1] Four days later, a *Los Angeles Times*/Bloomberg poll found McCain beating Clinton by a 14-point margin, 50 percent to 36 percent, with 10 percent choosing "other" and just 4 percent undecided.[2] If we take the results of these two polls seriously, it's amazing to envision that twenty-three months prior to the election, more than nine in ten voters had already made up their minds about which candidates to support. Even more amazing is the 21-point swing in voting preference in just half a week among what were supposedly decided voters. For some unfathomable reason, in the midst of their holiday shopping, with little news that could account for such a massive shift in opinion, millions of Americans who were intending to vote for Democrat Clinton suddenly changed their minds and rallied around Republican McCain.

McCain, however, had little time to bask in his good fortune. A week later, a CNN poll found the race dead even, with each candidate receiving 47 percent of the vote, other candidates receiving 4 percent, and just 2 percent undecided.[3] Here was either yet another massive shift in voter sentiment or a big red flag that there was something massively wrong with the polls.

Remarkably, those were not the earliest readings of the electorate's intentions for the 2008 presidential election. By the 2006 midterms, virtually all of the major media polls had already tapped into the presumed long-term ruminations of the general electorate. The earliest was reported by a Fox News/Opinion Dynamics poll in mid-November 2004, barely a week after Bush's reelection, showing Rudy Giuliani in a landslide victory over John Edwards, 50 percent to 38 percent—and just 12 percent undecided.[4]

These results make clear not only how useless are the early polls, but also how profound is the media's abhorrence of the undecided voter. Media pollsters will do everything they can to beat such a voter into oblivion, so they can begin horserace coverage long before the racetrack has even opened. But that is only one side of the story. To hedge their bets, the media will also admit that early polling numbers could easily change as the campaign progresses. Yet even as they say many voters haven't made firm decisions, these same news organizations will present poll results again and again that show only a small proportion of undecided voters.

In the spring of 2007, the Gallup editors provided a noteworthy exception to the pattern of ignoring voter indecision. In their analysis of "Where the Election Stands," based on a March poll, they noted that only 14 percent of voters said they had made up their minds, whereas three-quarters of the voters said they didn't have a good idea of which candidate they would vote for in 2008.[5] These are perfectly reasonable numbers, given how early it was in the election cycle. But looking at other poll results, including those of an earlier Gallup poll, you'd never know that so many voters hadn't made a choice. In fact, Gallup had reported in July 2006, eight months earlier, that hypothetical match-ups between John Kerry and Rudy Giuliani and between Kerry and John McCain had in each case revealed *only 3 percent of voters undecided.* [6] (Each of the Republicans won, 54 percent to Kerry's 41 percent, with 2 percent of respondents choosing "neither.")

So how were Gallup editors able to report an overwhelmingly decided electorate both before and after the March 2007 poll revealed a mostly undecided electorate? By using the phrasing that George Gallup had made an industry standard for preelection surveys: How would the respondents in those polls vote "if the election were held today"? Essentially the question says to respondents, Ignore the fact that you likely don't have the slightest clue who you'll vote for two years down the road—we want to know which candidate you're thinking about *right this minute.* To the respondents who dare to volunteer that they haven't been thinking about any candidate, typically the interviewer will follow up by asking if they "lean" toward any candidate, thus helping to reduce that awful "undecided" number. By contrast, in the March 2007 special poll, Gallup wanted to know the true state of the electorate's decision and therefore asked specifically whether respondents had made up their minds, not who they would support "today." In that format, large numbers of people told the simple truth: they hadn't yet decided.

Contrary to the approach of this special Gallup poll, pollsters justify "forcing" the respondent to choose a candidate by saying that tactic produces the most accurate election prediction. People may think they are undecided, pollsters argue, but in reality most voters usually at least lean toward a candidate, and in the election they are more likely than not to vote for that person. This is a dubious assumption for polls right before Election Day, but for polls weeks and months before the election, the notion that the forced-choice question produces good predictions is laughable. In fact, pollsters will always defend their polls when they don't make accurate predictions by arguing that the polls are just snapshots of the state of public opinion at one particular time. But if that's the case, early campaign polls should tell us how many voters are undecided about the choice they will make on Election Day. Pollsters can't have it both ways—arguing that their polls are only snapshots of one moment in time, while simultaneously airbrushing away the undecided vote and claiming this tactic helps to predict the future.

Pollsters should also give voters more credit. When people say they are undecided, especially a long time before an election, they actually mean it. If pressed, as they are in polls, voters will name a candidate, because they are being cooperative and playing the polling game, a game that requires active participation in the form of an answer. Otherwise, why participate in the poll in the first place? But for many respondents, these forced answers reflect only the shallowest of preferences—if indeed they are preferences at all—influenced by the latest news item, a passing comment from a friend, or even what name they happened to have heard most frequently. Respondents know that giving a response in the poll does not mean they are at all attached to that view. That's why pollsters acknowledge that early survey results reflect mostly "name recognition" rather than a serious choice by the voters.

It was clearly name recognition that explains why the early polls for the 2008 presidential campaign found John McCain and Hillary Clinton as the "early front-runners" for their respective parties—they were simply better known than their competitors. By the time the first nomination contest began in Iowa in January 2008, the media had long since written off McCain's candidacy and crowned Giuliani as the dominant Republican front-runner. The media still had Clinton as the Democratic favorite, but they would be shocked to discover in the five days that included both the Iowa caucuses and the New Hampshire primary that there was no Democratic front-runner. All those early polls had been wrong.

IN JUNE OF 2007, I was disappointed to read the latest results from a New Hampshire Primary poll, conducted by a University of New Hampshire colleague of mine, Andy Smith, director of the UNH Survey Center, for WMUR-TV (a local station) and CNN. Smith reported, among other findings, that just 2 percent of likely Democratic primary voters and 8 percent of likely Republican primary voters had not made up their minds. This was more than six months before the primary election, and we both knew how ridiculous those figures were. It was clear to Smith and me, in part because of our own experience talking with scores of well-informed voters in the state, that it simply wasn't true that 98 percent of the Democrats and 92 percent of the Republicans had made a meaningful choice. I suggested that on the next poll he include a question up front about whether the respondents had made up their minds and *then* ask the forced-choice question on candidate preference. That would allow the news media to get "normal" horserace figures but would also provide better insight into how committed voters were to their top-of-mind preferences.

Smith talked the idea over with CNN's polling director, Keating Holland, with whom I had worked collegially for years when CNN was Gallup's polling partner. Fortunately, Holland liked the idea despite the fact that the new procedure would deviate from what other pollsters did and possibly would open the network to criticism. He and Smith came up with a three-prong question: "Have you definitely decided who you will vote for in the New Hampshire Primary, are you leaning toward someone, or have you considered some candidates but are still trying to decide?" That seemed to describe the way most people viewed the status of their voting decision, but still there was a concern that by asking the question before the candidate preference question, the stated preferences might be affected in a way that would make it impossible to trend with previous polls. Ultimately, Smith and Holland deemed the risk to be low (as did I, though my vote didn't count), and that the new "undecided" question could potentially be quite useful in providing another newsworthy dimension to voters' opinions.

When Gallup had asked its "undecided" question up front in March 2007, it was on a special poll that did not ask the standard candidate preference question. Like Holland and Smith, the Gallup editors had been concerned that if interviewers asked the standard vote preference question ("if the election were held today") after the "undecided" question, the results of the preference question might be affected by the fact that so many respondents would have just admitted that they were undecided. Would that cause respondents to back off from saying whom they would support "today," if they had just admitted they hadn't made up their minds whom they would support on Election Day? Apparently not, as Smith and Holland were to discover.

In July, the CNN/WMUR-TV/UNH Survey Center poll asked whether respondents had made a decision about the primary election, and then asked the standard vote question.[7] The responses to the first question showed that just 7 percent of Republicans and 10 percent of Democrats said they had definitely decided on their vote, whereas about a fifth of Republicans and quarter of Democrats leaned toward a candidate. That left a stunning 71 percent of Republicans and 64 percent of Democrats saying they were completely undecided. That a substantial majority of voters were undecided on whom they would ultimately support did not prevent them from giving a top-of-mind answer on the standard question of their choice for president if they had to vote "today." Just 9 percent of Democrats and 12 percent of Republicans expressed no opinion on that question.

The same approach was used in the next two months, and the September results seemed to confirm that support for Clinton was growing. Based on the standard vote-choice question, she led Barack Obama in New Hampshire by more than 2 to 1,

43 percent to 20 percent, with the other candidates trailing far behind. Only 11 percent of voters were undecided, assuming the vote were held "today." The news media referred to Clinton's "solid" or "commanding" lead in the state, giving the impression that the election was all but over. However, based on the "undecided" question, the poll also showed that 55 percent of Democrats had still not made up their minds, and just 17 percent had "definitely" decided which candidate to support. That information was barely mentioned in most news stories, if at all, in part because it seemed to contradict the vote-choice question. How could more than half of the electorate be undecided if nine of ten voters expressed a preference? The problem was even more acute on the Republican side, where 66 percent of voters were listed as undecided, though the horserace figures also showed nine of ten voters choosing a candidate. Given the apparent contradiction, the news media emphasized the horserace numbers and ignored the undecided vote.

The results could have been reported in a way that would highlight the electorate's uncertainty. In figure 7, the actual report of the poll results is shown on the left, with an alternative—but more relevant—depiction on the right. The horserace figures on the right reflect the preferences only of voters who said either that they had definitely decided which candidate to support or that they were leaning toward supporting one of the candidates. The 55 percent who said they were still considering the candidates are classified as the undecided group. According to these results, Clinton still enjoyed a lead over Obama, but by 14 points (24 percent to 10 percent) rather than 23 points. More important, these results more accurately reflected the true nature of the public's views at the time and demonstrated why Clinton's lead was neither "solid" nor "commanding." With more than half the electorate still thinking about their vote choice, a 14-point lead could easily disappear (see fig. 7).

The same pattern occurred in reporting the Republican data. As late as November 2007, Mike Huckabee was written

FIGURE 7

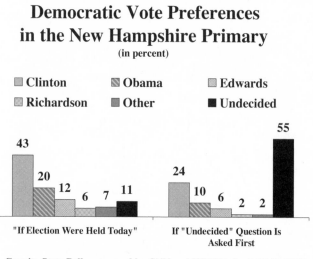

Democratic Vote Preferences
in the New Hampshire Primary
(in percent)

☐ Clinton   ▨ Obama   ▨ Edwards
▨ Richardson   ■ Other   ■ Undecided

Granite State Poll, sponsored by CNN and WMUR, Sept. 17-24, 2007

off as a serious candidate because he was getting only 5 percent of the vote in New Hampshire. The CNN/WMUR-TV/UNH Survey Center poll showed Mitt Romney with 33 percent, McCain with 18 percent, and Giuliani with 16 percent. Even dark horse conservative candidate Ron Paul, at 8 percent, was doing better than Huckabee. It appeared as though there was no hope for the Arkansas governor. But the first question in the poll also showed that just 15 percent of Republicans had "definitely" made up their minds and that 55 percent hadn't made even a preliminary choice. Television commentators seemed shocked in early December when Huckabee suddenly broke into the top tier of Republican candidates, with one pundit exclaiming, "He came out of nowhere!" It's times like these when the news media get hoisted on their own petard—after concealing the undecided vote, they're blindsided when voters finally make real choices.

One of the ironies of the experiment with the CNN/WMUR-TV poll is that CNN initially ignored the results of the "undecided" question. As a regular viewer of Wolf Blitzer's *The Situation Room*, I was dismayed to see no mention of the large percentage of undecided voters in New Hampshire when the poll results were announced in September. Then in early November, the UNH Survey Center conducted a poll for the *Boston Globe,* which included the same "undecided" question before the standard horse-race question, and with similar results. But unlike CNN, the *Globe* treated the figures seriously, with the headline: "Romney, Clinton Ahead, Vulnerable in N.H. Poll: Race Still Open, Analysts Say." The opening one-sentence paragraph reiterated that Romney and Clinton were front-runners but added that "vulnerabilities that could erode their support among voters in the weeks ahead." The next paragraph gave the horse-race figures, and the third paragraph informed the voters that "the primary contest in both parties remains highly fluid—just 16 percent of likely Republican voters said they had definitely decided whom to back; among likely Democratic primary voters, only 24 percent are firm in their choice."[8] For some reason, *that* finally got Wolf Blitzer's attention. He showed the *Globe*'s poll results on his program, expressing amazement at how fluid the vote was. Had he paid attention to the results of CNN's own poll a month and a half earlier, he could have scooped himself.

Surveying under a Lamppost

At the end of January 2008, just after Rudy Giuliani finished a poor third in the Florida primary and withdrew from the presidential contest, the *New York Times* published an analytical article with the headline, "For Giuliani, a Dizzying Free-Fall."[9] The authors recounted how his campaign "took impressive wing last year," that "voters seemed to embrace a man so comfortable wielding power, and his poll numbers edged higher to where he held a broad lead over his opponents last summer." So what happened? The polls were wrong. Giuliani never was the front-runner. The authors of the *Times* article seemed to recognize that possibility. "Perhaps he was living an illusion all along," they wrote. Perhaps, indeed.

Hillary Clinton and her supporters were living a similar illusion. The polls showed her as the front-runner among Democrats nationally, holding a commanding lead that ballooned to more than 20 points. A Gallup news release as early as May 2007 noted that she was "solidifying" her lead among Democrats.[10] In the period leading up to the Iowa caucuses, many political observers noted that she was running a national campaign against Giuliani, as though she were already the Democratic nominee and he the Republican opponent in the general election. That strategy proved a bit premature as her so-called solid lead evaporated immediately after she lost to Barack Obama in Iowa. Once again, the news media wondered, what happened? And once again, the answer was: the polls were wrong.

The problem with the apparent front-runner status of both Giuliani and Clinton is that it was based on national polls of Republicans and Democrats, respectively. These are people who don't vote—at least not all in the same primary election, and maybe not at all. The fact is, there is no national primary. And there is no national primary electorate. Whether candidates will do well in the contest for their party's nomination depends initially on their electoral support in the early caucuses and primaries, which are all state elections held at different times and with different candidates (since the less successful candidates drop out of the later state contests after doing poorly in the early ones). Polling a national sample of Democrats and Republicans reveals nothing about the dynamics of the state-by-state nomination contest. If pollsters want to measure the actual strength of candidates' support, they have to poll in each state separately—in Iowa, New Hampshire, Nevada, and South Carolina, among the states to hold the earliest elections. That approach is expensive, and the results often ambiguous, because voters are notoriously undecided in the early election contests and because it's never clear how much influence a victory in one state will have on the electoral fortunes of candidates in other states.

The ambiguity of the candidates' relative strength in the early part of a presidential election campaign is a nightmare for journalists, who cover the presidential elections like they cover sports. They need to know who is winning and who is losing, and who might surge and who might collapse. So pollsters long ago helped simplify the process by introducing a wholly fictitious entity—the national primary electorate. This is a convenient fiction, because the major media polls routinely conduct national polls on other issues. All they have to do to create that fictitious national primary electorate is ask Republicans and Democrats in their national samples which candidates they support for their respective party's presidential nomination. And voila! They can cut through all the complexity of the serial state elections by discovering what the made-up national primary electorate has to say.

Once the preferences of this fake electorate are measured, the numbers have a life of their own—no matter how irrelevant they are for describing the state-by-state electoral strength of the candidates. More important, those numbers are accepted as truth, even by people who should know better. It's an amazing tribute to the power of those poll-generated fabrications that Giuliani, who in the fall of 2007 didn't lead in any of the early contests—not in Iowa, or Wyoming, or New Hampshire, or Michigan, or South Carolina—could be considered the dominant Republican front-runner. Or that Clinton, who had trailed John Edwards in Iowa for months and was at best competitive in the later preelection polls in that state, would be credited with having a "solid" lead.

THERE IS A SECOND WAY in which those national polls of Democrats and Republicans don't tell the truth. Candidate preferences are all measured using the forced-choice question

"Who would you vote for if the election were held today?" which we know manipulates respondents into coming up with a choice even if they haven't made a decision. When the national polls were taken in the late fall of 2007, the vast majority of party members nationwide had not been paying close attention to the election campaign and thus were even less committed to any one candidate than were the voters in Iowa and New Hampshire. By the late fall of 2007, the voters in those two states had all been exposed to extensive campaigning by the presidential candidates, and voter attention was relatively high. Still, as the UNH Survey Center poll showed, about half of the voters in each party primary in New Hampshire were still undecided. Consider how many more people would be undecided in the rest of the country, where voters had not been exposed to the intensive campaigning seen in Iowa and New Hampshire.

That fact was made abundantly clear in late November 2007, when a special Gallup poll asked its "undecided" question of Democrats and Republicans nationally, before asking which candidate respondents would support for their respective party's presidential nomination.[11] For several months leading up to that poll, Gallup and the rest of the media polls had been showing Giuliani with a sizable national lead over all of his Republican opponents. But the Gallup poll in late November, which explicitly measured how committed voters were to any of the candidates, showed that the fictitious electorate was not nearly as engaged as poll results suggested.

A side-by-side comparison of Gallup's mid-November poll with its special late November poll finds two different worlds (see fig. 8). The *standard* Gallup horse-race question in mid-November found Giuliani with a 9-point lead over second-place Fred Thompson, 28 percent to 19 percent, with McCain getting 13 percent of the vote, Romney 12 percent, Mike Huckabee 10 percent, Ron Paul 5 percent, the rest 5 percent, and just 8 percent undecided. The *special* Gallup poll two weeks later, when one would expect to find more voters committed to a candidate,

FIGURE 8

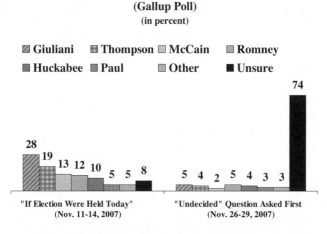

Republican Vote Preferences Nationally

(Gallup Poll)

(in percent)

revealed that 74 percent of Republicans nationwide had not made a decision, and that none of the candidates got more than 5 percent of the vote. Giuliani was not the front-runner—no one was. Had pollsters been willing to measure the undecided vote, they could have reported how little support *any* candidate had at that time rather than perpetuate the fiction that Giuliani was the man to beat.

The comparable figures for the national Democrats showed Clinton as a front-runner, but with only 18 percent of the vote, compared with 7 percent for Obama, 4 percent for Edwards, 1 percent or less for the other candidates—and 69 percent undecided. With so many voters sitting on the fence, it was clear that Clinton's national lead was far from solid. Several weeks later, when Obama won the Iowa caucuses, the phoniness of that lead was exposed for all to see.

I BELIEVE THAT in their heart of hearts, most media pollsters realize that the national primary electorate is bogus. What they try to do is put a positive spin on what is a convenient, if meaningless, exercise. A prime example comes from the *Washington Post* pollsters in an article showing Giuliani and Clinton as the early front-runners as early as December 2006:[12]

> These early poll results largely reflect name identification among the field of candidates, which includes several political celebrities and many others who remain generally unknown to people outside their states. As a result, hypothetical matchups are often poor predictors of what will happen once the primary and caucus season arrives in early 2008, and as voters learn more about where candidates stand on important issues.

Translation: The national primary polls are worthless. Of course, that can't be the pollsters' official position, or there would be no justification for doing the polls. So, having just said their own poll results don't provide much of a predictive insight into what will happen in the primary season, the authors reverse course in the next sentence to say, "But the findings provide early clues to the shape of the presidential nomination battles." They want it both ways—to acknowledge what experience tells them, that the polls don't provide much insight as to what might happen; but also to justify doing the polls anyway because they provide "early clues" about the primary season. The two statements are contradictory, and the proof is in the clues they touted: that the Republican field would be dominated by Giuliani and McCain, and that Clinton was the dominant, even overwhelming, favorite among Democrats. The actual situation as the primary season was about to begin, just two weeks before the Iowa caucuses and three weeks before the New Hampshire primary, was quite different from what the clues suggested. Mike Huckabee and Mitt Romney were the candidates to beat on the Republican side, not Giuliani and McCain, although they were still in the hunt. For Democrats, no single candidate dominated the race, as Clinton, Obama, and Edwards were all competitive in Iowa.

The *Post's* polling partner at ABC, Gary Langer, made an even more forceful argument in favor of national primary polls. Writing in July 2007, he pointed to a letter from an unnamed colleague who argued that national surveys about the nomination are "close to meaningless," because they measure national preferences in what is really a series of state caucuses and primaries. That, of course, is my argument as well. Langer acknowledged the criticism—"It's a fair complaint, and a serious one"—but argued that ABC asks the horse-race question primarily for context, "to see how views on issues, candidate attributes and the public's personal characteristics inform their preferences."[13] The problem here is that if the views people express have no bearing on the process, who cares what factors influence the irrelevant preferences of a fictitious electorate? More important, both ABC and its polling partner, the *Washington Post,* use the numbers in their news coverage not primarily for "context," but to characterize who's ahead and who's behind. Both news organizations continually referred to Giuliani and Clinton as the front-runners based on results from the national polls. One example from ABC was the October 3, 2007, headline "Clinton Advances, Strong in Base; Giuliani's Lead Has Less Oomph." The story was all about the leaders in the national poll and why they enjoyed significant electoral advantages.

ABC was not alone. Virtually all political observers were deluded by the polls of national Democrats and Republicans. There was hardly a journalist or political commentator or even a pollster during the fall of 2007 who didn't refer to Giuliani as the front-runner, while frequently treating Clinton as though she were the de facto Democratic nominee. If these national polls were not to be taken as predictive of these candidates' electoral success in the primaries, then the pollsters didn't take their own advice.

In a September 2007 column, CBS's polling director, Kathleen Frankovic, addressed the issue, but with more caution.[14]

She acknowledged that the lesson she had learned from past experience was "not to put too much trust in national polls as predictors of primary outcomes." But she, like Langer, still argued that the national polls provided the means to look at underlying factors—to compare differences between the general population and possible primary voters, and to "gather clues about the possible composition of the primary electorate." Again with those clues. The obvious response is that if pollsters want to show how primary voters differ from the general public and what factors influence their candidate preferences, pollsters should conduct polls in the early state contests, not poll people nationally who haven't even thought about the candidates.

In early December, almost as a testimony to the meaninglessness of the national primary polls, three major media organizations reported starkly different pictures of Clinton's front-runner status in the national primary electorate. All three were conducted within the time frame of December 5 through 9, precluding timing as a factor in the differences. CNN showed Clinton leading Obama by 10 points, CBS and the *New York Times* reported Clinton with a 17-point lead, and ABC and the *Washington Post* had Clinton leading by 30 points. Langer addressed the conflicting results, pointing to differences in the way each of the polls defined the national primary electorates and managed their samples (the number of interviews concluded per night). He implied that the ABC/*Washington Post* poll may have been the most accurate because it included an oversample of blacks, who tend to vote disproportionately for Clinton. But his final advice echoed his previous cautions: "Cut back on fixation with the horse race and look at the underlying evaluations."[15] Nice try—but shifting blame to the readers for *their* "fixation with the horse race" was hardly a defense for these disparate results. Besides, if the polls were wrong on the horse race, why wouldn't they also be wrong on the underlying evaluations?

THE MEDIA'S INSISTENCE on conducting the national primary polls is reminiscent of the joke about the drunk who lost his keys down the block, but searched for them under the lamppost because that's where the light was. A similar impulse seemed to be behind an announcement in late January 2008—just as Giuliani's candidacy proved how foolish it was to make any predictions based on a fictitious national primary electorate—that Gallup was now conducting *daily tracking polls* of this very same electorate, interviewing about a thousand Democrats and a thousand Republicans nationally every day on their presidential primary preferences. "These national numbers are a critically important indicator of the political environment when voters in more than 20 states go to the polls next Tuesday,"[16] wrote Gallup's Frank Newport. As it turns out, he was wrong. The Gallup Poll's national numbers showed Clinton up by 13 points, when in fact on Super Tuesday Clinton and Obama received about the same number of votes—essentially a dead heat. In response to a blogger on pollster.com who noted the "egregious" error, Newport quickly backtracked: "We never reported the Daily Tracking results as projective of what would happen on Super Tuesday."[17] It's true he didn't use those precise words, but the words he did use—that the numbers constituted "a critically important indicator of the political environment" for Super Tuesday—hardly seemed more accurate. Then, three weeks later, leading up to primaries in Texas, Ohio, Vermont, and Rhode Island, Gallup ended up dueling itself. Its daily tracking showed Obama leading Clinton nationally by 12 points, whereas its new poll with *USA Today,* conducted over the same period as the tracking poll, had Obama with only a 2-point lead nationally. There was no clear explanation for this discrepancy. As Mark Blumenthal noted on pollster.com, "Newport seems to be stumped."[18]

Gallup was not the only polling organization that kept showcasing this fictitious electorate, though it certainly invested many more resources into this effort than did any other organization. Virtually all of the major media polls continued to report on the national presidential primary preferences well after Super Tuesday, even though by that time, the nomination contests were all about the actual number of delegates each candidate was winning. In the same week that Gallup produced two contradictory results about the national Democratic electorate, two other national polls of Democrats also came up with conflicting findings: the *New York Times*/CBS News poll reported Obama leading Clinton by 16 points, whereas the AP/Ipsos poll had Obama with only a 3-point lead.[19] ABC's Langer suggested that one explanation for these otherwise incomprehensible findings was that "attitudes are simply unsettled."[20] Newport had a similar explanation: "There is a lot of volatility out there among Democrats."[21] Well, yes. Probably. But then the polls should have found large numbers of undecided respondents—and they didn't. However divergent their findings on the candidates, all the polls agreed that just 5 percent to 6 percent of the respondents had not made up their minds.

As these major media polls continued their mismeasurement of the fictitious national primary electorates, it was hard to fathom why anyone would take them seriously.

And the Winner Is . . .

Following the 2004 presidential election, the National Council on Public Polls posted a review of the final predictions of the many polls that interviewed people up to a few days of the election.[22] According to the report, "The 16 national presidential polls conducted in 2004 for the media had a very good year." Their average error on either of the two presidential candidates was less than 1 percentage point (.9 percent). Eleven of the polls had Bush ahead, four had Kerry in the lead, and one had the race tied. In addition, there were 198 state polls measuring presidential, gubernatorial, and U.S. senatorial races. The average candidate error in those polls, 1.7 percent, was about twice the average candidate error in the national polls but still quite small. Overall, only 9 polls out of 198, about 5 percent, could be considered "wrong." And that is precisely what is expected according to probability theory. Ninety-five percent of the polls should be within the margin of error, 5 percent outside.

Overall, this has to be considered a positive report on the ability of polls to estimate election outcomes when the polls are conducted close to Election Day. By that time, the standard horserace question—who would the voter support if the election were held today—comes close to congruence with reality, since the election is almost "today."

Given the agreement of the polls in predicting the winners, one could reasonably expect that different polls would give similar readings in the weeks leading up to the November 2004 election. Yet a graph of eight of the major polls during the month of September, after the two party conventions formally nominated their presidential and vice presidential candidates, tells a different story (see fig. 9).

FIGURE 9

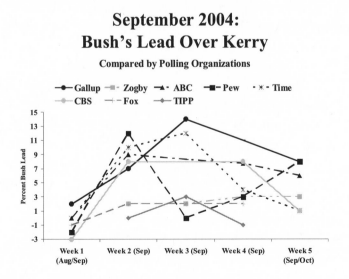

September 2004:
Bush's Lead Over Kerry

Compared by Polling Organizations

At the end of August and into early September, the CNN/ *USA Today*/Gallup poll showed Bush with a lead of 2 percentage points, whereas the CBS/*New York Times* poll had Kerry up by 3 points. That is the smallest gap between the high and low estimates of the different polls for September. The largest gap occurred in midmonth, with Pew calling the race as tied and CNN/*USA Today*/Gallup saying Bush had a 14-point lead. After that point, Pew and Gallup went in opposite directions, meeting each other at the end of the month with an eight-point lead for Bush.

While most major polling organizations showed Bush ahead by 5 to 8 percentage points by the end of September, the stories they told about the electorate during the month varied wildly. Gallup showed a big surge for Bush, then a slight decline. Pew showed a bounce up, a bounce down, then a bounce up again. Fox found no early bounce for Bush at all, and a consistently close race. Like Gallup, *Time* had a big early surge for Bush, but then saw his numbers fall to a much lower level. ABC recorded a modest surge, but then little change thereafter. What, then, to make of such conflicting numbers? "Anybody who believes these national political polls are giving you facts is a gullible fool," wrote Jimmy Breslin of *Newsday*. "Any editors of newspapers or television news shows who use poll results as a story are beyond gullible. On behalf of the public they profess to serve, they are indolent salesmen of falsehoods."[23]

Contradictory poll results also occurred during the 2000 election campaign. In a postelection article, Pew's Andrew Kohut noted the fairly accurate predictions of the polls right before Election Day but also their poor performance during the campaign. "But being accurate in the end," he wrote, "did not improve the image of polling in a campaign that was tarnished by too many horse-race polls that confused rather than clarified public opinion."[24] He went on to note the sharp fluctuations in results, especially with Gallup's tracking poll, which he said "produced loopy results that defied credibility." Rich Morin of the *Washington Post* had earlier railed against Gallup and other polls, noting that depending on which of nine major polls one might read, George W. Bush was leading Al Gore by anywhere from 3 to 20 points. "Already it's been a silly season of statistical goofs and gaffes," he wrote, "perpetrated in the name of news by clueless journalists and the pollsters who accommodate them."[25]

Neither Morin nor Kohut, however, zeroed in on the major reason why there are fluctuations in the polls. They point to quick polls with small samples, which necessarily mean larger margins of error. And there is some truth to those charges. But they ignore what I think is a far more pervasive factor—the way media polls measure voters' preferences. By forcing respondents to choose a candidate in the interview, even though they may not have made a decision, polls measure a "vote" that for many people has no real meaning. The closer we get to the election, the fewer the meaningless votes, which results in less fluctuation. But in the meantime, the polls mislead us as to what the electorate is really thinking—making the vote appear more volatile than it really is, and completely ignoring the very real fact that many people use the information generated by the campaigns to come to a decision. In the twenty-one polls that Gallup conducted between March and October 2004, the percentage of respondents who were recorded as being unsure varied between zero and 3 percent. If we believe Gallup, there were virtually no undecided voters during the whole of the election campaign, though there was tremendous fluctuation in the recorded vote.

The contradictory picture that polls paint of a highly volatile, though completely decided, electorate raises credibility problems for polls more generally. Everybody knows many voters are undecided early in a campaign and then make up their minds as election day nears. In 1996, Gallup departed from its normal routine and asked up front whether voters had made up their minds—the same question that was asked in March 2007.

But in 1996 it was asked much later in the campaign, at the beginning of September—even then, four out of ten voters said they had not yet decided which candidate they would support.[26] Yet, we never see anything like that number in the standard polls reported by the media today.

ANYBODY WHO WANTS to know how candidates are faring during an election will be hard pressed to find any polls that reveal the truth about voter sentiment. They all use the forced choice format to measure candidate preferences and suppress any measure of indecision. Ultimately, that format will produce a fairly accurate estimate of the election outcome if the question is asked shortly before Election Day, because by that time most voters have made up their minds. But in the weeks and months and years before the election, these polls give a misleading, even false, picture about the electorate. Regrettably, problems that polls have in describing public opinion during election campaigns are just compounded in polls about public policy.

CHAPTER FIVE

Misreading the Public

The great promise of public opinion polls was not that they would be able to predict election winners, but that they would give voice to the people between elections. That at least was the hope of George Gallup when he launched "America Speaks" in the early 1930s, and it remains the universal vision of media pollsters today. The question from the beginning of modern polling, however, has always been the same: How well do the polls measure what people are thinking? Election predictions can be checked for accuracy against the electoral results, but there is nothing comparable against which to measure the accuracy of the typical public policy poll. Pollsters try to establish their overall credibility by demonstrating how well they can predict elections, the assumption being that if they are successful there, they must have good samples that represent the American public on more general policy issues. That's not necessarily a good assumption, of course, since even in election campaigns the polls are not especially reliable in describing the public mind.

Beyond the credibility of the pollster, there is another, though still imperfect, way to assess the potential accuracy of a public policy poll—whether or not it agrees with other polls asking roughly the same question at roughly the same time. If they all agree, it doesn't mean they are all right. They could all be wrong in the same way. But if the polls disagree with one another, we definitely know that at least one is inaccurate. Comparisons over the past several years suggest some real problems with public policy polls, which are increasingly more likely to confuse than they are to enlighten us about what Americans are thinking.

One of the major problems is that opinions on public policy are more complex than those expressing a vote choice. A single question will rarely suffice, because there are so many facets of any given policy. Moreover, the policy may be so arcane, or the public so unengaged in the issue, that large numbers of Americans have no opinion about it at all—a fact that media pollsters generally do everything in their power to conceal. Rather than allow respondents to freely acknowledge they don't have an opinion, pollsters pressure them to choose one of the available options. Respondents in turn try to come up with some plausible reason for choosing one answer over another. If they don't have much information about the issue, they pick up cues from the way the question is framed or from other questions in the survey. The net result is that many respondents are influenced by the questionnaire itself.

An extreme example of how drastically polls can manipulate public opinion occurred shortly after President Bush's re-election, when he announced that he would try once again to have Congress pass legislation to permit oil drilling in Alaska's Arctic National Wildlife Refuge (ANWR). A national poll released by Republican Frank Luntz in January 2005, on behalf of the Arctic Power interest group, found a public that supported oil drilling in ANWR by a margin of 17 percentage points (51 percent to 34 percent). Yet in direct contradiction, a similar poll conducted December 13 through 15, 2004, by John Zogby for the Wilderness Society found the public opposed to oil drilling in ANWR, by the exact same margin (55 percent opposed to 38 percent in favor).[1]

It seemed more than coincidental that the poll results happened to conform with the desires of the sponsoring organizations. And a look at the questionnaires shows how easy it was to shape the findings into mirror opposites. Luntz preceded his question on oil drilling with 13 questions that dealt with the cost of oil and with energy dependence on foreign countries. By the time the interviewer got to the question of exploring and developing oil reserves in ANWR, many respondents were primed to solve the country's energy needs by opening up that area to the oil industry. Zogby, on the other hand, framed the issue in a less biased way, asking only one question related to the oil industry before the drilling question. But that one question helped present the issue as an environmental matter, and in that context a solid majority of the respondents opposed oil drilling.

A key to understanding how easy it was to manipulate respondents into giving the desired answers is recognizing that most people had little knowledge about ANWR going into the survey. Eighty-seven percent of Luntz's respondents, for example, could not say where the Arctic National Wildlife Refuge is located—the same percentage could not accurately identify even one word of the acronym ANWR. In addition, only 8 percent said they knew either a lot or a good deal about the area. Despite this lack of knowledge, only 7 percent of Zogby's sample and 15 percent of Luntz's sample declined to offer an opinion. Clearly, information presented over the course of the interview helped many respondents form an instantaneous opinion.

Although the contradictory results make it difficult to specify what the "true" state of public opinion was, there are some useful indicators. Even a biased poll in favor of oil drilling found 34 percent opposed, and a biased poll opposed to oil drilling found 37 percent in favor—suggesting a mostly divided public, with a substantial proportion not having a deeply held opinion. But there were no intensity questions, so we don't know how engaged the public was—how many people had a deeply held view compared with how many expressed top-of-mind opinions.

A Gallup poll in March 2005,[2] just a couple of months after the Zogby and Luntz polls, tried to get at that intensity dimension when it first asked a neutral question: "Do you think the Arctic National Wildlife Refuge in Alaska should or should not be opened up for oil exploration?" People were opposed 53 percent to 42 percent, with just 5 percent unsure. The follow-up question asked respondents if they would be upset if what occurred was the opposite of what they had just said they preferred. The result was that 19 percent of respondents wanted oil drilling and would be upset if it didn't happen, 45 percent were opposed and would be upset if it did happen, and 36 percent essentially didn't care. Among those who cared, opposition to the proposal was greater than 2 to 1, but there's a catch. The question was asked after numerous questions on global warming and on the ability of various government agencies to protect the nation's environment. In that context, the intense opposition measured by Gallup among its respondents might well be greater than among the public as a whole.

Unlike the other two polls, the Gallup poll on oil drilling in ANWR was not sponsored by a group with a vested interest in the results. Having worked on that specific Gallup poll myself, I can personally attest to the fact that we did not intend to bias the results. The poll itself was part of Gallup's monthly Social Series surveys, which measure public opinion about various matters regularly. In January of each year, for example, Gallup devotes a poll to measuring the mood of the country, in February to public opinion on world affairs, in March to the environment, in April to the economy, and so on. Because there are so many questions related to the environment in the March poll, it would be impossible not to ask some questions after respondents had already heard several about the environment. Inevitably, the early questions will influence how some respondents answer the later ones. Generally, the more questions on the environment, the more likely respondents are to give environmentally positive responses as the interview continues.

The Luntz and Zogby examples illustrate how pollsters are often treated as guns-for-hire. In each case, the policy question itself was neutral, but the questionnaire context of each poll was manipulated to produce the desired results. Find the right pollster, get the right answer. This is not to say that on every topic, polls can produce whatever a sponsoring organization might want. But on topics about which most people know very little, enormous swings in results can easily be obtained by careful questionnaire designs.

The Gallup example illustrates what's wrong with most media polls that purport to measure an objective public opinion. Though it did the measure the intensity of the expressed opinions, it failed in several other areas. There was no attempt to measure how much people knew about the issue, and the question was posed in a forced-choice format. Whether avoidable or not, the ANWR question was asked after several other questions about the environment, which clearly biased the answers of respondents who had been unengaged on the issue before the survey. And no attempt was made to discover why people supported or opposed the oil drilling. George Gallup wanted his polls to provide a guide for political leaders, but the results of the Gallup poll in this case were hardly useful for that purpose.

New Democratic Congress and the Bush Surge

On February 13, 2007, members of the U.S. House of Representatives debated a historic nonbinding resolution that would soon put the House on record as opposing President Bush's troop surge in Iraq. The Speaker of the House, Democrat Nancy Pelosi, who was guiding the resolution through the legislative body, invoked the public on behalf of her cause: "The American people have lost faith in President Bush's course of action in Iraq, and they are demanding a new direction."[3] The president, meanwhile, had begun the phased deployment of 21,500 more troops to Iraq, a move for which he similarly claimed public support.

If ever there was a time for pollsters to help inform political leaders as to what the public was thinking, this was it. The Democrats had just stunned the nation by regaining majority control in both the House and the Senate, largely—though not solely—on an antiwar campaign. In what can perhaps best be described as an ironic interpretation of the election, President Bush announced that he had listened to the voters, and what he heard was that Americans wanted "change" in the war's direction. So, he would effect that change by temporarily *increasing* the number of U.S. troops in Iraq, a "surge" that would take place over the next several months. The Democrats' interpretation of the voters' will was, understandably, at odds with the president's. After all, the exit polls showed that only 17 percent of voters wanted to send more U.S. troops to Iraq, while 55 percent wanted to withdraw some or all of the troops. Still, once Bush decided to send more troops, the question for pollsters became whether or not the public now supported the congressional Democrats in passing a resolution condemning the president's actions. Pelosi explained exactly what such a resolution would mean: "No more blank checks for President Bush on Iraq." But would the public rally around what seemed to be a promise to stop funding the troops in Iraq?

The public opinion polls on this question offered little insight (see fig. 10).[4] Two polls by CNN found that a two-to-one majority of Americans wanted to pass such a resolution.[5] In mid-January, the USA *Today*/Gallup poll also found a large majority in favor, but by a somewhat smaller majority.[6] Then in February, the USA *Today*/Gallup poll changed its wording and found a mostly divided public, slightly leaning toward support.[7] Two polls by CBS, one in late January and the other in early February, found a deadlocked public.[8]

The differences in poll results weren't due to timing, but

FIGURE 10

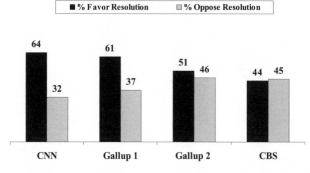

Support for Non-Binding Resolution
Against Bush Surge In Iraq
Jan-Feb 2007

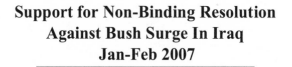

to question wording. CBS got virtually the same results in both January and February after asking identical questions in both polls. Likewise, CNN got essentially the same results with the same question in two different polls in January. Gallup's two contradictory findings, on the other hand, came after a major change in wording between the first and second round of questioning. Whatever the differences in wording, the three polling organizations presented two conflicting results: the public was either largely in favor of the resolution, or the public was about evenly split.

Many critics felt that a nonbinding resolution was not sufficient. Instead, if Congress wanted Bush to stop the war, then Congress should just refuse to fund it—an authority granted by the U.S. Constitution. At the heart of the issue was what the public understood "stopping funding" to mean. Some people thought it meant the troops would not have the clothes and food and war supplies they needed to protect themselves, while many others assumed that blocking funding would translate to the troops returning stateside. Here too the polls provided scant clarification of what the public was thinking (see fig. 11). CNN

FIGURE 11

Support for Blocking Funding To Oppose Bush Surge In Iraq Jan-Feb 2007

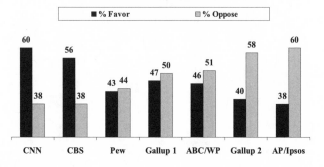

and CBS showed overwhelming support for withholding funding, whereas Gallup and AP/Ipsos reported the exact opposite. Three other polls showed a public that was about evenly divided. Once again Gallup had the distinction of producing two very different results, as it again changed its question wording between its mid-January and mid-February polls.[9]

The normal excuses for the differences—timing, question wording, and question context—are hardly persuasive. There were only slight, nonsignificant changes over time for the organizations that conducted two or more polls using the same question wording, so timing cannot explain the contradictions. A careful examination of the questions suggests some of the differences are ascribable to question wording and question order, especially for the two Gallup polls, but there is no obvious explanation for the mirror opposite results of CNN at one end of the spectrum and AP/Ipsos at the other end. It's significant that none of the polling organizations admitted that its poll was wrong, though it's obvious that some must have been. If the pollsters can't or won't tell us which numbers best reflect the public will, political leaders certainly aren't in any position to do so.

The truth is that probably none of the polls gave an accurate picture, because none examined what people believed it meant to block funding. Nor did the polls make it easy for respondents to say the question was too ambiguous and they didn't have an opinion. Instead, in a rush job, the polls squeezed the public to come up with opinions that ultimately told us little about the public's reaction to stopping funding.

A similar phenomenon occurred in the case of a proposal to set a timetable for the withdrawal of troops from Iraq. The Bush administration vehemently opposed setting any kind of a timetable, but the Democrats in Congress insisted on making such an effort. In March and April of 2007, five different polling organizations weighed in with their reports on the public will. Where one organization conducted more than one poll asking the same question, there were no significant differences from one poll to the next, suggesting no change in the public's mind over a two-month period. But the results among polls from different polling organizations were not as consistent.

CBS showed a large margin in favor of Congress's setting a timetable, by 32 points; whereas Gallup found a much smaller margin of 22 points; NBC/*Wall Street Journal,* 19 points; and Pew Research, 18 points. The ABC/*Washington Post* poll found an almost evenly divided public, showing a 3-point margin in favor of timetables.[10] Pollsters may point to the consensus among four of the polls that a substantial majority was in favor of timetables, but the 14-point difference between CBS and Pew is far greater than the polls' margins of error. The two polls were telling two very different stories. And then there's the ABC/*Washington Post* poll, contradicting the other four by reporting a sharply divided public on the issue, rather than one that was widely in favor of the timetables.

These results illustrate another problem with the media polls as they superficially try to cover a wide range of issues, all the time forcing many respondents to come up with opinions they haven't fully developed. The issue of setting a timetable for withdrawing troops was just one strategy for pressuring Bush, and not one that most Americans had necessarily spent much time considering. If they did support the timetables—and we don't know for sure given the contradictory polls—it was undoubtedly more of a general support for scaling back the war in Iraq than a specific commitment to timetables. Ultimately, given their lack of a super majority in the U.S. Senate and the opposition of Republicans, congressional Democrats were unable to set meaningful benchmarks or timetables. As for what the public wanted, that remains a matter of controversy among the pollsters.

SIX MONTHS AFTER President Bush pushed through the troop surge in Iraq, Congress received a report from the U.S. commander in Iraq, General David Petraeus, on the success of the troop increase. It was working, he said: violence had declined. He expected to be able to reduce the number of U.S. forces back to pre-surge levels by the summer of 2008. Part of the news story was public reaction to this report, but once again the polls could not agree over what Americans were thinking.

The sharpest difference came when the CBS/*New York Times* poll arrived at the opposite conclusion from the *USA Today*/Gallup poll, even though both were conducted over exactly the same time frame, September 14 through 16, 2007. The CBS website ran the headline, "Poll: Most Say Bush Iraq Plan Falls Short." The opening sentence presented the gist of the findings: "Most Americans continue to want troops to start coming home from Iraq, and *most say the plan President Bush announced last week for troop reductions doesn't go far enough.*"[11] By contrast, the Gallup website reported a more upbeat public. "Gen. Petraeus Buys Time for Iraq War, but Not Support" was the top headline, with a smaller headline that directly contradicted the CBS findings: "Most Americans side with the level and pace of Petraeus' proposed troop reductions."[12]

CBS arrived at its conclusion after telling respondents that the Bush proposal for reducing troops would bring the number of U.S. troops to the pre-surge level by the summer of 2008. After getting that information, 50 percent said more troops should be withdrawn by that time, whereas 36 percent said the reduction was either the right amount or too great. Gallup told its respondents that Bush was adopting Petraeus's recommendations for troop reduction but did not say what they were. Then it asked whether the troop reductions were too little, about right, or too much "based on what you have heard or read about this plan." In this context, Gallup got the opposite of the CBS results—51 percent saying the reduction was about right or too great, and 36 percent saying the reduction was too small.

Here we have two of the most prestigious polling organizations in the country, employing state-of-the-art methods for measuring the public mind, yet one found a large majority opposed to the size of the Petraeus force reduction, and the other found a large majority in support. In truth, most respondents probably knew little about the issues they were supposed to judge, instead relying on what they were told in the course of the interview to make snap judgments. The pollsters went along with the charade, concealing public inattention to the matter and pretending the opinion they had just measured precisely described the American public.

Sending Troops to War

There are few actions by a government that are as profound as sending troops into combat or deciding how long to keep them in a war zone. But if political leaders were looking to the public for guidance from 2003 to 2005, they didn't find much help from the ABC/*Washington Post* and CNN/*USA Today*/Gallup polls. By amazing coincidence, the two polling organizations conducted surveys in 2003, 2004, and 2005 that overlapped each other in the dates of interviews and focused on the exact same topics, yet came to opposite conclusions each time as to what a majority of Americans wanted to happen.

In July 2003, the question was whether the United States should participate in a peacekeeping force in Liberia. One might expect large numbers of Americans to excuse themselves from offering an opinion on the grounds that they didn't know why such troops would be needed in that country, but both media polls found few respondents willing to admit ignorance. The ABC/*Washington Post* poll showed opposition to such a venture by 10 points (51 percent to 41 percent), whereas the CNN/*USA Today*/Gallup poll showed a 21-point margin in favor (57 percent to 36 percent). Ironically, the only thing the polls agreed on was a suspiciously small number of "unsure" respondents—8 percent and 7 percent, respectively.[13]

In April 2004, the issue was whether Americans wanted to send more troops to Iraq. The ABC/*Washington Post* poll said they did, 54 percent to 44 percent, whereas Gallup and its polling partners reported the public as saying not only no, but hell no! The tally was 62 percent opposed and 33 percent in favor.[14]

In June of 2005, the Iraq question was reversed: Did the public want the United States to begin to withdraw troops from Iraq? Gallup said it did, by a small majority (51 percent to 44 percent), whereas ABC/ *Washington Post* said the public was definitely opposed by a substantial majority (58 percent to 41 percent).[15]

I should point out that in each case, the questions asked by the polling organizations were somewhat different, and those differences could probably help to explain why the polls came to opposite conclusions. In the case of a peacekeeping force to Liberia, however, it was probably more a matter of question context. Before asking about Liberia, the ABC/*Washington Post* poll asked several questions about the situation in Iraq, such as whether American forces were getting bogged down there. It's quite possible by the time the interviewer asked the peacekeeping question, the unengaged respondent looking for cues in the questionnaire was conditioned to look askance on military ventures. No such questions preceded the Gallup question on Liberia.

Frank Newport, editor in chief of the Gallup Poll had a different perspective on the reasons for the different poll findings. Writing in a blog, he noted:

> There are other subtle differences between these questions, but the bottom line is probably the fact that Americans know little about Liberia. The Gallup Poll shows that only 10 percent are following the situation there very closely, while 53 percent aren't following it closely. *Opinions about sending in U.S. troops are therefore very dependent on how the case is made in the questions and what elements of the situation there are stressed to them* [the respondents].[16]

This was an unusually candid admission for a pollster to make: that both ABC/*Washington Post* and the Gallup Poll essentially manufactured the public opinion they reported. They "made the case" for the issue differently in the two polls, and they stressed different "elements of the situation," giving rise to two very different opinions—neither of which told the truth about how little people knew and how unengaged they were from the issue.

Closer to Home

While large numbers of Americans are not attentive to foreign policy, and thus not likely to have formed meaningful opinions about such issues, we would expect more people to be tuned in to domestic matters. And that's certainly the case. Still, even on issues covered widely by the press, many people are not informed enough to make a reasonable judgment. That doesn't bother media pollsters, of course, who generally gloss over or outright conceal the public's lack of attention to domestic policies in order to generate public opinion fodder for their news stories.

Since 1997, the federal government has been administering the State Children's Health Insurance Program (SCHIP), which helps states pay for health insurance for children of low-income parents who nonetheless make too much to qualify for Medicaid. In 2007, a new bill would have renewed the program and expanded it to cover about 3.8 million more uninsured children at a cost of $35 billion over the next five years. The expansion would be effected by raising the limit of income a family could earn to qualify, and the cost was to be covered by an increase in the cigarette tax. President Bush vetoed the measure because he said it was a step toward socialized medical care, and he insisted that the program would encourage parents who could afford insurance to use SCHIP instead.

The issue seemed to be one that could affect the presidential election—if not in the primaries, then at least in the general election. And so it was no surprise that several media polls decided to measure the public's reaction to the proposal.

It is a complex policy, so it would not be unwarranted to find out how much people knew about the proposal before asking them whether they favored or opposed it. But of the four media polls that measured the public's views on this issue in late September and October of 2007, only Gallup included a question that measured attentiveness. The Gallup poll showed that about half of the public was not following the story and that just 17 percent said they were following it very closely. No doubt most pollsters suspected at the outset that relatively few people would know the details of such a complex policy, yet they decided against measuring and reporting ignorance.

The low level of public attention meant that the polls had to feed respondents information about the proposal if they were going to come up with something newsworthy. And indeed, they all did tell respondents something about SCHIP. The only trouble was, they all fed respondents different information and consequently wound up with wildly varied results (see fig. 12).

In fact, there were four different readings of the public's views on SCHIP, three showing large margins in favor of expansion, and one poll showing a clear majority in opposition.[17] The CBS results were the most positive, showing 81 percent in favor, followed by 71 percent found by the ABC/*Washington Post* poll, 61 percent by CNN, and 40 percent by Gallup. A close reading of the specific questions can help explain some of the differences among the polls, but the major conclusion is that *each poll provided a reading that was significantly different from every other poll*. If these polls had been measuring the horse race in a political campaign, all would have been tossed out as garbage. They weren't garbage, of course. Each provided some kind of insight into public opinion, or at least what that opinion *might be* if all Americans were informed about the issue in the exact same way that poll respondents had been.

The CBS poll, for example, was the tersest in its explanation, saying that a government program currently provided health insurance for "some low-income families," before asking

FIGURE 12

Public Support for SCHIP
Sep - Oct 2007

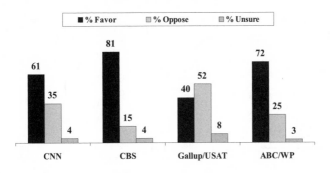

if respondents would favor expanding the program "to include some middle-class uninsured children." That sounded so positive—with no mention of cost, for example—that it's surprising anyone said no.

Gallup, by contrast, fed its respondents much more information. It first described the bill as one that "would increase the number of children eligible for government-subsidized health insurance." "Government-subsidized" has a pejorative connotation, just as "welfare" sounds more negative than "assistance to the poor." It's surprising that Gallup used this terminology, because the editors there are typically very conscientious about avoiding such inflammatory language. Also, whereas CBS did not mention the partisan divide, Gallup noted that "the Democrats want to allow a family of four earning about $62,000 to qualify for the program, while President Bush wants most of the increases to go to families earning less than $41,000." Which "side," Gallup asked, did respondents favor—the Democrats' or the president's? Later, critics pointed out that the information was highly selective and misleading, not mentioning the number of uninsured children who would be helped and implying the Democrats wanted most of the assistance to go to families earning $62,000 a year, which wasn't the case at all.

CNN also emphasized the partisan conflict, noting that "President Bush vetoed a bill passed by Congress that would create a program to spend $35 billion to provide health insurance to some children in middle-income families." Did the respondents want Congress "to create that program by overriding Bush's veto" or to "block that program by sustaining Bush's veto?" The question implied that overriding the veto would "create" a *new* program and that Bush wanted *no* program, when in fact he was opposed only to the expansion of an existing program. But after hearing the issue cast as a partisan conflict, most people wanted to override the veto.

Like the CBS poll, the ABC/*Washington Post* poll mentioned nothing about the conflict between Democrats and the president. It told respondents the proposal would increase funding by $35 billion over the next five years and would be paid for by raising the cigarette tax. The question also noted that supporters claimed the program would provide insurance for millions of low-income children, whereas opponents said the program would cover children in families that could afford insurance. Mentioning the cost no doubt elicited a lower level of support than what CBS reported but still higher than what CNN found when it emphasized partisan conflict. And ABC/ *Washington Post,* like CNN, implied that the choice was between the whole program (including the expansion) and no program rather than a choice between the current level of support and a higher level.

Because only Gallup showed majority opposition to the proposed expansion of SCHIP, its numbers prompted a flurry of blogging and an essay on the website pollster.com from Emory University political science professor Alan Abramowitz about the "biased" wording of Gallup's questions.[18] Abramowitz wrote that he preferred the ABC/*Washington Post* poll wording, but he neither addressed the shortcomings of that question nor mentioned the fact that feeding *any* information to respondents taints the samples. Gallup's senior editor, Lydia Saad, wrote a response to Abramowitz's criticism acknowledging that the Gallup question mentioning the different income levels could have "confused the respondents," but she added that none of the polls, in her view, did an adequate job of probing what the public really wanted. Although noting that only about half of the public was paying some attention to the issue, she maintained that "Americans clearly have some opinions worth tapping," and concluded that the challenge to pollsters "is to probe further for a more thorough and accurate understanding of whether Americans would rather have the existing program that covers families earning up to twice the poverty level, or whether the program should be expanded to include families earning more than that."

She was right, of course. None of the polls (including her own organization's) made that distinction about the choice between the current SCHIP and the proposed expansion of SCHIP, which was at the heart of the controversy. More important, none of the polls could legitimately claim to represent the general public because each poll fed its respondents selected information, which the general public did not have. The real public, where only half of Americans knew anything about the program, wasn't represented in these polls at all.

ABORTION IS ONE of the most fiercely and frequently debated social issues in the United States, so one might expect that most people would have an opinion on it, and probably a strong one at that. But even on this highly divisive issue, pollsters disagree on what Americans want.

The question in recent years has been whether it should be easier or more difficult for women to obtain an abortion.[19] It only complicates the issue further when we get conflicting public opinion data on abortion not only from different polling organizations, but even from the same one. When Pew Research was polling for its religious forum in July 2006, it found only 31 percent who said abortion should be generally available, whereas 66 percent wanted to make it more difficult for women to obtain an abortion. Of that 66 percent, 11 percent favored a complete ban on abortions, 20 percent wanted stricter limits in general, and 35 percent favored a ban with exceptions only in cases of rape, incest, and danger to a woman's life.

Yet four months earlier, when Pew was polling for its general news release, which was *not* part of its religious forum, it found that only 37 percent favored making it more difficult for a woman to get an abortion and that 56 percent were opposed. The question wording was different in the two polls, and although one might reasonably attribute the differences in results to the framing of the questions, the net result is that Pew produced two highly contradictory results within a very short period of time, with no accompanying explanation as to which was the more valid reflection of the public will. Clearly both could not be right.

In the same time frame, Harris found that 40 percent favored making it more difficult to secure an abortion and that 55 percent were opposed. A CBS/*New York Times* poll in January 2006 found that 60 percent wanted access to abortion to be more limited and that 38 percent held the opposite view.

These results suggest that even on an issue which has received an overwhelming amount of news coverage over many decades, many people have not formed a stable opinion (see fig. 13). The issue is just not salient to such people, and they may be especially susceptible to being influenced in their poll responses by the questionnaire itself. But media polls typically make no effort to differentiate between people who have strongly anchored views on the issue and people who do not. Who will tell the country's political leaders which of these pictures is the one they should respect? And which of its conflicting results will Pew stand by?

FIGURE 13

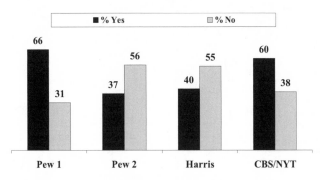

Should it Be More Difficult to Obtain An Abortion in This Country?

(January – July 2006)

There are countless other examples of media polls misrepresenting the public because they force people to express opinions that are neither well informed nor deeply held. After Bush's reelection, dozens of polls showed wildly different opinions about the president's proposal for private retirement accounts funded from Social Security payroll taxes. Gallup alone found opinion ranging from a 28-point margin of support to a 15-point margin of opposition, depending on the way the question was asked. In January 2005, the ABC News/*Washington Post* poll reported the public in *favor*, 54 percent to 41 percent, of a plan that would reduce the rate of Social Security growth but allow a stock market option. In the same month, a *Wall Street Journal*/NBC News poll reported the public *opposed*, 56 percent to 33 percent, to a plan that would gradually reduce guaranteed Social Security benefits in exchange for workers' being allowed to invest some of their Social Security payroll taxes in the stock market. Though the plans were phrased in similar terms, one poll found a 13-point margin of support, the other a 23-point margin of opposition.[20] Again, most people simply didn't know much about the issue, and forcing them to come up with an opinion in an interview meant that different polls ended up with contradictory results.

Even on matters that are very personal, on which pollsters may think that most people have formed some opinion, it's possible to influence attitudes. In December 2003, for example, a CBS/*New York Times* poll reported that Americans supported a constitutional amendment to ban same-sex marriages by a 15-point margin, whereas the highly respected Annenberg Center at the University of Pennsylvania found Americans opposing the amendment by a 12-point margin.[21] It doesn't take a math whiz to figure out that both polls couldn't be right.

COLLECTIVELY, THESE EXAMPLES call into question the validity of so many polls that claim to measure what the public is thinking. By manipulating Americans who are ill informed or unengaged in policy matters into giving pseudo-opinions, pollsters create an illusory public opinion that is hardly a reflection of reality. How often do media polls misread Americans on public policy matters? The answer, unfortunately, is almost always.

CHAPTER SIX

Damaging Democracy

No one can doubt the enormous power of media polls in American politics today. They are so widely viewed as revealing the will of the public that it may seem blasphemous to charge them with undermining American democracy. But the truth is that most of today's polls claiming to measure the public's preferences on policy matters or presidential candidates produce distorted and even false readings of public opinion that damage the democratic process. That was the case with the supposedly overwhelming public support for war prior to the invasion of Iraq, which I described in the beginning of this book. The special Gallup poll that scratched beneath the surface of people's whims found that the American public was in reality evenly divided—about three in ten favoring war, three in ten opposed, and the rest not caring one way or the other. Most polls did not report this truth about public opinion because they refused to measure the degree of uncertainty and apathy that existed among Americans. This even split among people who cared about the issue existed despite overwhelming pro-war news coverage and repeated reports of a hawkish public. Politicians who might have opposed the invasion or at least have demanded more evidence to justify a preemptive attack simply caved in to the media-created illusion of a nation gripped by war fever.

The Legitimacy Spin Cycle

It's crucial to recognize that the role polls play in serving the media's power bias is to provide closure to a cycle that legitimizes the policies of those in power. The cycle began, in the case of Iraq, with White House efforts to build a case for war starting almost immediately after 9/11. Subsequent events have shown those efforts to be replete with duplicity, including fake evidence suggesting weapons of mass destruction and an imminent threat from Iraq, along with repeated fear-mongering by various members of the Bush administration. The press then reported the "news" almost solely from the perspective of those in power.

In principle, reporters should seek numerous sources of information to present a wide variety of viewpoints, but in practice they rely mostly on government sources. That is particularly true with matters of foreign policy and war. The *New York Times* and the *Washington Post* later acknowledged that they should have given more coverage to opposing points of view during the run-up to the Iraq war, but at the time they and almost all of the other major news media organizations essentially acted as megaphones for the administration's viewpoint.[1] The Knight-Ridder chain was a major exception—the chain's thirty-one newspapers, including the *Philadelphia Inquirer,* the *Miami Herald,* and the *Detroit Free Press,* did in fact take a "hard look at the administration's justifications for war." Unfortunately, with no papers in New York City or Washington, D.C., Knight-Ridder's critical coverage was generally ignored by other mainstream media.[2] What most Americans saw in the news, therefore, was pretty much only what the administration wanted them to see. According to the media watchdog group Fairness and Accuracy in Reporting (FAIR), in the three weeks before the U.S. invasion of Iraq, only 3 *percent* of U.S. sources on the evening news of PBS and the five TV networks—ABC, CBS, CNN, FOX, and NBC—expressed skeptical opinions about the impending war.[3]

Overwhelmingly, the media's sources favored the invasion of Iraq, despite considerable disagreement among many experts outside the administration who saw major moral and logistical problems behind a preemptive strike, as well as a dearth of evidence that would justify it. After giving readers and viewers skewed reasons for such a serious undertaking, the media then conducted their polls to measure the public's top-of-mind reaction and discovered—surprise!—widespread support for the war. This gave the administration's position the stamp of public approval and completed the legitimacy spin cycle. In the case of the Iraq war, the cycle was more than a onetime series of events. The steady drumbeat of the polls, with their repeated illusions of war support, helped perpetuate the cycle by creating a national political climate that made it increasingly difficult for either the press or politicians to question the administration's push for war.

By the standards of today's journalism, reporters are unlikely to question the assertions of the president's administration outright, no matter how suspect those assertions might seem. Instead, to appear balanced, reporters need to interview sources outside the administration, typically members of the major opposition party. But as media scholar Lance W. Bennett and his colleagues note, "As the Democrats contemplated the spectacle of a well-spun media against the backdrop of a nation whipped to a patriotic frenzy, the impulse to raise critical questions or challenges to the impending war may have seemed politically suicidal."[4] This reluctance of Democrats to criticize the president in turn "deprived reporters of opposition voices to quote, and of hearings to cover."[5]

Had opinion polls shown the reality of a divided public, with a large number of Americans either unconvinced or unconcerned about the reasons for going to war, the national political climate almost certainly would have been quite different. It's likely that more congressional Democrats would have had the courage to raise objections, giving reporters more sources to advance their stories. But the polls didn't show the truth about the divided public, and, as a result, national public debate over the merits of the war was markedly constrained. Having caved in so easily at the beginning of the war, members of the media and Congress found it easy to do so again a year later.

ON APRIL 28, 2004, CBS's 60 *Minutes II* showed horrific photos of Iraqi detainees being abused and tortured at Abu Ghraib prison. Immediately after the broadcast, the Bush administration and its supporters claimed the actions at the prison were aberrations, isolated incidents perpetrated by a few soldiers in violation of explicit U.S. policy. The administration also launched an intensive campaign to convince the public that, while there was mistreatment of prisoners, possibly even abuse, nothing that occurred at Abu Ghraib constituted torture under international law and the Geneva Convention.

The national debate over what happened at Abu Ghraib and whether or not it was part of a broader U.S. policy supporting harsh and possibly illegal treatment of prisoners and suspected terrorists could have had a major effect on the 2004 presidential election. Reporters had a wide variety of sources not sanctioned by the Bush administration who could have provided additional information on the issue.[6] The Red Cross and numerous human-rights organizations, for example, had documented similar actions by the U.S. military and CIA operatives in American-run prisons abroad, both inside and outside Iraq. There were also publicly available military reports that indicated that many of the problems at Abu Ghraib could be found in other U.S. detention centers. The press also had access to government memos that explicitly condoned the use of harsh tactics against suspected terrorists. Yet overall, the mainstream media relied principally on what members of the Bush administration told them about Abu Ghraib. As Bennett and his colleagues note, "The few early questions about whether the photos revealed a new torture policy were soon lost in the volume of reported claims by the administration that Abu Ghraib was an isolated case of low-level 'abuse.'"[7]

The fact that U.S. policy not only condoned but even encouraged the use of torture did not become widely acknowledged until the end of the following year, long after the 2004 presidential election. At that time, Sen. John McCain broke with the Bush administration by introducing an amendment to the 2005 defense appropriations bill that outlawed torture. The amendment passed the Senate with a vote of 90 to 9. In the meantime, media polls continued to report that the public accepted the administration's claims that the abuse at Abu Ghraib was isolated and did not constitute torture. Given how closely the polling questions mirrored the administration's position, it's not surprising they found widespread public agreement.

The ABC/*Washington Post* poll conducted two major surveys shortly after 60 *Minutes II* broke the Abu Ghraib story. In both polls, one conducted in early May and the other two weeks later, the questionnaire referred to "apparent abuse" of prisoners by U.S. soldiers, rather than to "torture," a term the Bush administration vehemently opposed. The CNN/*USA Today*/ Gallup poll likewise refrained from using the administration's verboten word but was willing to use the term "abuse" without the qualifier "apparent." In late June, the CBS/*New York Times* poll used more neutral language, referring to the "treatment" of prisoners. That same month, the NBC/*Wall Street Journal* poll asked respondents about the "torture and abuse" at Abu Ghraib, the only poll to do so.

The ABC/*Washington Post* poll asked some of the most extensive questions about Abu Ghraib. The headline of the May 5–6, 2004, report on ABC's website reassured the administration that those calling for drastic redress, like the firing of the secretary of defense, were way off base: "Most Are Dismayed by Prisoner Abuse, But Few Call for Rumsfeld's Resignation."[8] ABC and the *Washington Post* noted that a little more than a third of respondents had been following "very closely" the news reports about the "apparent abuse of some Iraqi prisoners by American soldiers in Iraq," whereas a quarter of the public was essentially clueless. The rest were "somewhat" aware. No matter their degree of awareness of the story, all respondents were asked a series of forced-choice questions about the issue. By a two-to-one majority, respondents said that the incidents were isolated, not widespread. And a three-to-one majority (69 percent to 20 percent) said that Defense Secretary Donald Rumsfeld should not resign.

In the May 23–25 follow-up poll, ABC/*Washington Post* found a substantial increase in the percentage of people who disapproved of the way Bush was handling "the issue of the apparent abuse of Iraqi prisoners by U.S. soldiers"—57 percent, up from 35 percent two weeks earlier. More important, the poll found that most Americans accepted the administration's point of view that what happened at Abu Ghraib was *not* "torture." That finding, however, was almost a foregone conclusion because of the way the poll questionnaire was designed. Prior to the key question asking for their views, the interviewer referred to the Abu Ghraib incidents three separate times as "apparent abuse" of prisoners and once as just "abuse" of prisoners, before asking respondents: "Do you think what Americans soldiers did to prisoners at the Abu Ghraib prison in Baghdad amounts to torture, or do you think it was abuse but not torture?" Sixty percent said "abuse but not torture," and only 29 percent called the actions "torture."[9] After having just been told four times by ABC that the actions were "abuse," what's amazing is that three out of ten respondents still said "torture."

Though the ABC/*Washington Post* poll reported only a third of Americans following the scandal "very closely," Gallup found a slightly more attentive public—four in ten paying close attention, and two in ten mostly oblivious to the issue, with the rest "somewhat" attentive. Again, regardless of how closely they were following the issue, all respondents were asked a series of forced-choice questions about Abu Ghraib. Though most respondents were concerned about the abuses, they still felt, two to one, that the incidents were "isolated" rather than "common occurrences." Overwhelmingly, they believed the soldiers violated U.S. policy (79 percent)—thus exonerating the Bush administration—and also that the soldiers were acting on their own (56 percent) rather than following orders (34 percent). And similar to the ABC/*Washington Post* poll, Gallup found a two-to-one majority saying Rumsfeld should not resign.[10] These were exactly the findings the White House had campaigned for since the scandal first came to light. The polls reinforced the administration's narrative that the actions at Abu Ghraib were of minor significance, the unlawful acts of just a few soldiers and certainly not indicative of some larger problem. The forced-choice questions had elicited positive opinions from people who could not possibly have known how widespread the incidents were nor whether they were part of a systematic Department of Defense torture policy. Had they been given the option, it's possible most people would have admitted that they did not know enough to offer a view. Instead, pollsters depicted a highly informed and supportive public, which could then be used to tell the press and Congress to back off because the people were on the president's side.

As senior editor of the Gallup Poll at the time, I participated in the design of the Gallup questionnaire. I certainly had no intention of abetting a spin cycle initiated by the Bush administration, but in retrospect I see how clearly my colleagues and I fulfilled that function. We used "abuse" because that was the prevailing term, set by the administration, of course, but also widely adopted by the mainstream news media. Using the term "torture" would have constituted a judgment call, one that conflicted with the language reporters were using on CNN and in *USA Today*. There was simply no chance we would take an approach different from that of our media partners. That wasn't our job. Finally, we asked forced-choice questions, rather than offer a "don't know" option, because our media partners wouldn't have found it interesting to report that large portions of the public had no opinion on the matter.

Unfortunately, our actions were part of a pattern that is almost inevitable given the current paradigm of poll reporting. With their self-imposed subservient role and acceptance of journalistic standards of what is "news," pollsters cannot help but be part of the legitimacy spin cycle. Those in power frame the issue to favor their position, the press limits its coverage of sources that might disagree with the administration and also directly mimics the framing to avoid appearing biased, the pollsters in turn develop surveys to dovetail with the news stories, and the people—many of whom have little idea of what is happening—are pressured into answering questions that reinforce the original positions of those in power.

IT'S IMPORTANT TO NOTE that the legitimacy spin cycle is nonpartisan. Republicans have been in the White House for the past two presidential terms, so the examples thus far show how polls have tended to help them. But during President Clinton's time in office, the same phenomena occurred. Perhaps the most dramatic instance occurred in the aftermath of the FBI's raid of the Branch Davidian religious sect's compound in Waco, Texas. On February 28, 1993, the Bureau of Alcohol, Tobacco, and Firearms (ATF) had stormed the compound, leading to the deaths of four ATF agents and six members of the sect. A temporary truce followed. The FBI then laid siege to the compound for 51 days. During its final assault on April 19, fires broke out in the compound. Overall, seventy-six Davidians were killed, including twenty-one children.[11]

Questions arose as to whether FBI agents, who had propelled tear gas into the compound, had also used pyrotechnics, which could have caused the lethal fires. Critics also questioned whether Attorney General Janet Reno should have delayed the attack. The initial uproar among elected officials in Washington and the press quickly died down, however, when poll results two days later revealed that the public was overwhelmingly behind the Clinton administration's actions. Having just joined the Gallup Organization in March, I was surprised at how much influence Gallup's one-night poll seemed to have on the political climate in Washington.[12] The poll found that only a quarter of Americans were paying close attention to the standoff, another quarter were paying no attention, and about half were following the issue "somewhat" closely. Regardless of awareness, only 13 percent of all respondents thought the FBI should have waited any longer to assault the compound. Overall, 87 percent blamed the cult's leader, David Koresh, "a great deal" for the resulting deaths, and just 16 percent had the same view about the FBI. Only 37 percent thought the earlier raid by ATF agents was irresponsible. And 83 percent thought it appropriate for "federal authorities to take action against the Branch Davidians, based on what the authorities believed was happening there."

The lesson here is that in April 1993, the legitimacy spin cycle worked to the Clinton administration's immediate advantage. The quickie poll, concluded within 48 hours of the assault, showed overwhelming support for the FBI's actions among people who hadn't even had time to discover the details and got the Clinton administration off the hot seat. Although there were two internal investigations, by the Treasury and Justice Departments, an independent investigation was not initiated until years later, when Attorney General Reno appointed former senator John Danforth as a special counsel to investigate the events. In the meantime, we at Gallup thought we had done a real service to the country by "letting the people be heard." The notion that we had manufactured a public consensus to serve those in power never crossed our minds.

IT'S NOT ALWAYS the case that media polls act to legitimize the positions of those in power. Sometimes they misinform the democratic process by exaggerating public support for one position or another on issues that are vigorously debated in society. In August 1999, I wrote an article for the Gallup website about the public's support for creationism.[13] A CNN/*USA Today*/Gallup poll conducted two months earlier had found that 68 percent of Americans supported "teaching creationism *along with* evolution in public schools," while just 29 percent disagreed. My release was posted shortly after the Kansas Board of Education's decision to downgrade the teaching of evolution in public schools, thus seeming to suggest that the decision was in accord with the American public. CNN and *USA Today* also published the findings. One evangelical organization, Answers in Genesis, was so pleased with the results that it announced them in its international newsletter.

The problem with the poll, as pointed out by public opinion scholar George Bishop, was that it failed to determine if respondents even knew what creationism was. He cited the results of another poll the following November, conducted by the Daniel Yankelovich Group, which showed that about seven in ten Americans had little to no familiarity with creationism. Despite this massive ignorance, the Gallup poll was able to "force" 97 percent of respondents to weigh in on the issue. Gallup accomplished that feat by asking the question as part of "a variety of proposals concerning religion and public schools." It was the twenty-ninth question in the poll, and by then respondents knew the name of the polling game—the faster they answered the questions, the faster they would get through the interview.

The question itself was general, not asking whether creationism should be taught in science classes, but whether it should be taught at all. And, of course, Gallup did not include an intensity question to determine whether people were just spouting top-of-mind responses or were imparting cherished principles. The net result, according to Bishop—and I agree with his assessment—was that "once more, a press release by a reputable polling organization had created a highly misleading impression of American public opinion."[14] We at Gallup should have explored the issue in more depth, but instead we used a single question to do a bad job of assessing public opinion on a complex issue. In the process, we contributed more to fueling propaganda than to furthering our understanding of the public.

Unfortunately, this is an all-too-frequent approach among media pollsters studying Americans' opinions on public policy issues. Bishop cites numerous examples in his book on *The Illusion of Public Opinion*,[15] but one can look at almost any area on pollingreport.com and spot the same two problems. First, people are rarely asked how much they know about a topic or how closely they have followed an issue in the news. Second, respondents are generally asked forced-choice questions that pressure them into giving an opinion. The result is the impression that, on most issues, the public wants a given outcome, when in fact so much of the public is unengaged that there isn't a majority either way. But that isn't interesting news, so pollsters report manipulated results as though they represent the will of the public. And these numbers in turn affect the political environment and even the legislative process.

The Bogus Preelection Polls

The biggest problem with preelection polls is that people believe them. Naturally, the most fervent evangelists for news media polls include the news media, which base stories on horserace numbers; and the politicians, who shape their campaign strategies with an eye to those same numbers. There are skeptics, of course, who will denounce contradictory poll findings or point out the egregiously wrong polls that crop up from time to time, especially during the primary season. The problem is that, almost immediately, a new set of poll numbers will change the focus from what was wrong with the old polls to what the new ones have to tell us about the public.

Bogus preelection polls were probably the single most important factor in creating Rudy Giuliani's bid to become the 2008 Republican Party's presidential nominee. His high poll numbers among Republicans nationally, even as late as mid-December 2007, were almost universally accepted as prima facie evidence that he was the front-runner for the nomination. Chief among those deluded by the polls was his senior policy advisor, Anthony V. Carbonetti, who told the *New York Observer* three months before Giuliani's withdrawal from the race without having won a single delegate, "I don't believe this [the nomination] can be taken from us. Now that I have that locked up, I can go do battle elsewhere."[16]

Most problematically, the news media not only believe the polls but use them to evaluate which candidates deserve to be covered. The whittling-down process hurts the candidates who are screened out since they don't get the coverage they need to increase their name recognition, stimulate contributions, and attract voters to their campaigns. Their inability to jump-start their campaigns in turn justifies the original decisions of the media not to cover them. This self-fulfilling prophecy starts with poll results that are deliberately manipulated to give the impression of clear front-runners even when there aren't any.

The screening process was evident in John Edwards's campaign for the 2008 presidential election, which typically received less news coverage than either Barack Obama's or Hillary Clinton's. In December 2007, FAIR posted an Action Alert [per website] that said, "*USA Today* Squeezes Edwards Out of Race."[17] The Action Alert took issue with *USA Today*'s article on the importance of electability to the Democrats. According to the article's author, Susan Page, "Democratic voters increasingly are focused on nominating the most electable presidential candidate, a USA Today/Gallup Poll finds, and Illinois Sen. Barack Obama fares better than New York Sen. Hillary Rodham Clinton against prospective Republican rivals."[18] What bothered FAIR was the exclusion of John Edwards from the discussion, since several polls had shown that Edwards was as electable, if not more so, than either Clinton or Obama. And FAIR had a point.

Electability is typically tested by pitting each of the top Democratic candidates against each of the top Republican candidates in hypothetical match-ups for the general election. In early December, CNN provided the most extensive match-ups of polls at that time, including four Republicans and three Democrats.[19] The results showed that Edwards was the only one to have a lead over McCain, by 8 points; Obama was in a tie, and Clinton trailed by 2 percentage points. Edwards's leads over Huckabee and Romney were 10 points or greater than the leads recorded for Clinton and Obama. Against Giuliani, Edwards led by 9 points, Obama by 8, and Clinton by 6. (See fig. 14.)

Just a note here to clarify what these figures mean. While I oppose the media's use of national polls of Democrats, and sep-

FIGURE 14

Among Democratic Candidates, Only Edwards Led All Republican Candidates in General Election Match-ups

(CNN Poll, Dec. 6-9, 2007)

	The Lead Enjoyed by Democratic Candidates Over Republican Candidates		
	Clinton	Obama	Edwards
Against Giuliani	Led by 6	Led by 8	Led by 9
Against Huckabee	Led by 10	Led by 15	Led by 25
Against McCain	Trailed by 2	Tie	Led by 8
Against Romney	Led by 11	Led by 13	Led by 22

arately of Republicans, to determine the front-runners for each party's presidential nomination, the national polls of hypothetical general election match-ups do relate to a real-world event —the actual election in November. That's why pollsters consider it legitimate to conduct these national poll match-ups, to get a preview of how the election might turn out once both parties have chosen their nominees. I believe such early polls are typically worthless, and can in fact do as much harm to the democratic process as the early preprimary polls, when they are used to suppress the truth about the electorate. Nevertheless, in principle, general election match-up polls at least are trying to describe a future real-world event, and are often used by pollsters and politicians to predict the electability of potential candidates.

In this context, it seems obvious from CNN's match-up that in any electability discussion about the Democratic candidates in mid-December 2007, Edwards should have been a prime focus. CNN's poll results had been published several days before USA Today/Gallup began interviewing, and there were other polls also showing Edwards to be at least as electable as Clinton and Obama. But USA Today and Gallup decided that Edwards was not poll-worthy; they made the same judgment about McCain among the Republican candidates. In the USA Today/Gallup poll, Clinton and Obama were each pitted against Giuliani, Huckabee, and Romney.

The exclusion of Edwards is noteworthy because at the time he was highly competitive in the Iowa caucuses, eventually coming in second there behind Obama. Apparently, his major sin was trailing Clinton and Obama in the bogus national primary polls. It's typical that the news media in general use these national primary polls to guide their election coverage. That doesn't mean they slavishly follow the latest figures, but it does mean that a candidate who is trailing in such polls suffers in news coverage. That was clearly the reason why Gallup and USA Today decided Edwards was not worthy of analysis in their mid-December poll on electability. In Gallup's early December poll of Democrats nationally, Edwards was in third place, 9 points behind Obama and 15 points behind Clinton[20]— too far back, evidently, to be considered viable by USA Today and Gallup.

The irony here is that only two weeks earlier, Gallup showed how misleading the national primary figures can be. In a special poll, it abandoned the forced-choice format and instead asked all Democrats nationally if they had even made a decision about which candidate to support. Sixty-nine percent said they had not. Just 18 percent expressed support for Clinton, 7 percent for Obama, and 4 percent for Edwards.[21] Gallup itself headlined the ensuing report, "Nationally, Choices for Party Nominees Still Wide Open." Given such an overwhelmingly undecided electorate, and with Edwards trailing Obama by just 3 points according to Gallup's own poll, there was no justification for USA Today and Gallup to exclude Edwards in its subsequent poll.

Among Republicans, the CNN match-ups showed McCain as the most electable, but he too was excluded from the USA Today/Gallup poll. The rationale for his exclusion was based on the results of polling the fictitious Republican primary electorate, where he had dropped from competitive front-runner to also-ran. As with Edwards, McCain's exclusion seems indefensible given Gallup's own poll two weeks earlier, which showed 74 percent of Republicans undecided, and no discernible front-runner.

USA Today and Gallup were not alone among the media organizations to whittle down the actual field of candidates in each party by using the national primary polls to guide their coverage. Virtually all the polling organizations at the time were running only truncated general election match-ups, because the dominant media theme at the time was that the general election would almost certainly be between Clinton and Giuliani—a major embarrassment to the media polls, given the eventual outcome. More important, news stories were shaped around these expectations, which in turn had a significant influence on the ability of candidates to raise money and attract people to help in their campaigns. Mark Mellman and Mike Murphy, Democratic and Republican campaign consultants, respectively, reinforce this point when they warn that although the early polls don't provide useful information about what the voters are thinking, they do have an effect on the campaigns:

> The [poll] measurements themselves, printed in bold type on Page 1, create their own distorted results, inaccurately advantaging some while disadvantaging others. By creating a potentially illusory sense of momentum or of failure, these pseudo-measures affect the extent of media coverage, fundraising, endorsements and the willingness of volunteers to engage. The result is a cycle. Early national polling is used to declare winners and losers. Those declarations affect the flow of money and coverage, which is then reported as winners and losers, part two, thereby driving the next polls. In 2003, this cycle nearly buried Kerry.[22]

In 2008, this cycle clearly hurt John Edwards and John McCain —both candidates' coverage and fund-raising suffered because of their low standing in the fictitious national primary polls. Eventually, of course, McCain managed to recover, while Edwards was forced out relatively early.

WE CANNOT UNHINGE the news media from the polls. When it comes to the news media's addiction to polling, Chris Matthews of MSNBC's *Hardball* said it best, just after the New Hampshire primary: "We live by polls."[23] Despite such widely held views in the news media, there is no good reason that media polls have to create mythological publics and fictitious electorates, that they can't measure apathy as well as engagement, or that they shouldn't differentiate crystallized from top-of-mind opinions. Scholar Scott Althaus writes, "Opinion surveys might produce some negative consequences for democracy, but that should not prevent us from exploring whether there are better techniques of polling or more appropriate roles for surveys to fill."[24] Indeed, polling can be a useful tool for enhancing democracy, but only if it's used to serve the needs of the public, not the whims of the press.

CHAPTER SEVEN

Uncertain Future

On January 8, 2008, the date of the New Hampshire primary, media pollsters suffered their biggest failure in election prediction since the 1948 presidential contest, when the three major scientific polls of the day all confidently predicted Republican Thomas Dewey to beat incumbent Democratic president Harry S. Truman. At the time, expectation of a Republican victory was so pervasive, news stories analyzing what a Dewey administration would look like were being written days before the actual election.

A similar national consensus emerged in the days just before the New Hampshire primary, when pundits of all stripes across the country were predicting the demise of Hillary Clinton's candidacy in light of eleven different polls forecasting her almost certain defeat on primary day. On average, these polls showed Barack Obama winning with 38 percent to Clinton's 30 percent. Obama's lead varied from 3 percentage points, reported by Franklin Pierce College, to 13 points, reported by both Gallup and Zogby.[1] The stunning final vote count: Clinton won with 39 percent to Obama's 37 percent.

The magnitude of the pollsters' failure was highlighted by

ABC's Gary Langer, who referred to it as "New Hampshire's Polling Fiasco," saying that it was "essential" to have a "serious critical look" at those results. "It is simply unprecedented for so many polls to have been so wrong," he wrote. "We need to know why."[2] Langer's ABC News poll and its partner the *Washington Post* poll conducted a single survey in New Hampshire in early December but wisely avoided polling toward primary day, which meant that their poll results were too far removed to be compared with the vote count. Later Langer joked online, "What I like best about the final New Hampshire pre-election polls is that I didn't do any of them."[3]

Langer's call for a serious critical look at other news media's polls was shared by key members of the American Association for Public Opinion Research. Five days after the election, the association's president, Nancy Mathiowetz, announced the formation of an ad hoc committee "to evaluate pre-election primary methodology and the sponsorship of a public forum on the issue." After reassuring the public that polls have long been "remarkably accurate," Mathiowetz wrote that, "Sixty years ago the public opinion profession faced a crisis related to the poll predictions of the Truman-Dewey race. The way survey researchers reacted then—with a quick, public effort to identify the causes—played a key role in restoring public confidence and improving research methodology."[4]

Many pollsters and pundits attributed the New Hampshire meltdown to the long-standing problem of "nonresponse"—the increasing difficulty in reaching respondents who are willing to be interviewed. These days, more and more people screen their calls with answering machines and caller ID. Even if pollsters can get through, Americans are increasingly unwilling to participate. The question posed by "New Hampshire's Polling Fiasco" was whether pollsters simply hadn't been able to reach enough Clinton supporters—and whether this portended a terrible polling performance for the presidential election campaign.

For Many Are Called, but Few Are Interviewed

The nonresponse problem goes back to George Gallup's first efforts at polling the public. In the 1936 election, he discovered that Democrats were not as likely as Republicans to return mail ballots. Nonresponse was highly related to "economic strata"— higher income and better educated respondents were more likely to answer mail ballots, to be Republicans, and to vote for Alf Landon. The *Literary Digest* suffered from the same pattern of nonresponse. Even when it sent out ballots to *all* registered voters in certain areas, as it did in Allentown, Pennsylvania, for example, Landon voters were more likely to return the ballots. In Allentown, he got 53 percent of the *Digest's* vote but only 41 percent of the actual vote.[5]

Gallup's solution was to swear off mail ballots, and instead use only interviewers to ensure that voters of all economic strata were included proportionately in his samples. And for the next several decades, nonresponse was not a major problem. But by the mid-1980s, according to Eleanor Singer, a public opinion scholar and former longtime editor of *Public Opinion Quarterly,* pollsters noticed what appeared to be a severe decline in response rates.[6] This was a period when they were switching from in-person interviews at the respondents' homes to interviews conducted over the phone. One of the most prominent scholars of public opinion research, Howard Schuman, wrote that when he began polling at the University of Michigan in the 1960s, he routinely expected to reach at least 80 percent of the people he attempted to contact. The other 20 percent were split fairly evenly between those who couldn't be reached during the interview period and those who declined to participate. A success rate of less than 80 percent, he wrote, "was a dismal showing, throwing considerable doubt on the validity of results for the target population."[7] By the 1980s, such high expectations could no longer be met. And there were indeed mounting doubts about the validity of poll results.

Still, it wasn't completely clear whether response rates were declining because people were less willing to participate or simply because phone interviewing made it easier to refuse. For the next decade, pollsters studied the problem, including the rather difficult task of how to measure nonresponse accurately. By the early 1990s, pollsters were likely to get interviews with just 50 percent of targeted respondents. Some of the decrease was caused by more people declining directly, and some by people being inaccessible, although that undoubtedly included many indirect refusals—people who screened calls to avoid telemarketing calls and opinion surveys. Inaccessibility became much more common with the advent of answering machines and, at the end of the 1990s, caller ID, confounding pollsters about how many people were actually taking steps to avoid them and how many just weren't available at the time of the call.

Pollsters' initial reaction was to try to increase response rates, by improving interviewer training, and even providing monetary and other incentives to respondents to participate. The conventional wisdom was that the higher the response rate, the greater the likelihood that the sample would represent the whole population. That assumption was reasonable, assuming that eventually pollsters might come close to the high standards that Schuman was able to meet in the 1960s. But the reality was quite different. Response rates had plummeted so low, they would never recover. On any given project, pollsters might be able to improve the response rate by a few percentage points, perhaps even as much as 10 or 20 points, but often that still left a big gap. And new research suggested that, in some cases, these very efforts to improve response rates could make the sample *less* representative of the population as a whole. People who were likely to be influenced to participate by special incentives might be much different from those who were not tempted by the gift of a $2 bill, a special pen, a $5 check, the chance to be in a lottery, or some other small bribe. In that case, the more *some* people—and not others—were enticed by these incentives, the less representative the whole sample might become.

Researchers then shifted their focus from how to improve response rates to the more fundamental question of whether low response rates made any difference. Could samples do a good job of representing the larger population even though nonresponse was so high? The key is whether, for any given sample, the people who cannot be interviewed—either because they can't be contacted or because they decline the interview—are substantially different from the people who agree to be interviewed. If the differences in attitudes between these two groups is small, then pollsters can feel reassured that they are still able to conduct polls that provide valid information about what the larger public is thinking.

Pollsters Reassured or Deluded?

Two of the most widely cited studies that looked at the problem of low response rates were conducted by the Pew Research Center in 1997 and in 2003.[8] Like all studies of nonresponse, they were constrained by the fact that when people are not included in a survey, we have no way of knowing what their opinions are. The crux is this: We want to know if respondents are different from nonrespondents, but how do we know what the nonrespondents think if we can't interview them?

There is, however, at least a partial check on such a poll's validity. Typically pollsters compare the demographic characteristics of their samples with the U.S. census and with the annual current population survey (CPS) that is part of the census. Although the CPS is a poll (a very large poll nationwide, of about fifty thousand households a month),[9] it generally achieves response rates in the 90 percent-plus level, because it is government sponsored and people feel obligated to participate. Thus, the CPS demographic numbers provide the most reliable check on whether poll samples truly represent the

American public—as far as the distribution of age, gender, geographic location, race, and education are concerned.

The problem is that even if polls get a good cross-section of Americans in terms of demographic characteristics, they don't necessarily get a good cross-section of Americans in terms of their attitudes. People who refuse to participate in polls may be quite different in their opinions from people who give up their time to be interviewed, even though the two groups may be similar in age, gender, geographic location, race, and education. And *that* is the core of the nonresponse problem for pollsters. They simply don't know how good their samples are in representing the rest of the country. That's why the Pew studies provide an incomplete, but nevertheless, modestly useful approach to assessing the validity of polls. The researchers couldn't compare respondents with *pure* nonrespondents, since we can't know what people won't tell us. But Pew did compare a regular sample of respondents with a sample of people who were much harder to persuade to participate—people who in normal surveys would be excluded because they were too difficult to contact, or who initially said no and were not asked to reconsider their decision.

The "regular" respondents in the Pew study are those who were interviewed in what Pew calls a "standard" survey—interviewing conducted over a five-day period, with up to ten call attempts (if the initial call found a busy line or answering machine). The overall response rate was 25 percent, which meant that three quarters of the people Pew attempted to interview as part of its sample either refused or could not be contacted in the first place. By Schuman's standards of the 1960s, that's an atrocious outcome—but actually better than most media polls these days.

The second group of people in the 2003 Pew study was interviewed in a "rigorous" survey, which lasted more than 21 *weeks*—from the beginning of June to the end of October. The longer time period provided researchers the opportunity to make repeated callbacks to potential respondents, send letters to traceable addresses asking the potential respondents to participate, offer $2 incentives, and even attempt, two times if needed, to convert people who initially refused to change their minds. This group included many respondents who would not have participated had Pew not taken more than four months to wait them out and pressure them to complete the interview. One in seven of these respondents required twenty or more call attempts before completing the survey. The overall response rate of this rigorous survey was 50 percent—twice as large as the standard survey, but remarkably low given the extraordinary measures taken.

The authors noted that the response rates for 2003 were substantially worse than in 1997. In the earlier study, the standard and rigorous surveys each achieved response rates that were 11 points higher than the comparable rates in 2003. The major reason for the decline was the increased unwillingness of people to be interviewed. By taking 21 weeks to conduct callbacks on the rigorous survey in 2003, Pew was able to contact an amazing 91 percent of people they wanted to interview—not much different from what Pew accomplished in 1997. But only 58 percent of the people agreed to be interviewed in the later study, down from 72 percent six years earlier.

Still, the key focus of the study was on how representative the samples were of the population at large. Typically, national media polls underrepresent people in five categories: those who are younger, lower educated, Hispanic, nonwhite, and living in urban areas. Pew's standard survey was within a percentage point of the CPS figures on blacks, but it underrepresented people in the other four categories. The rigorous survey, compared with the standard survey, exacerbated the underrepresentation of younger people, significantly improved the representation of Hispanics, slightly improved the representation of lower educated people, and had little effect on urban underrepresentation.

The differences between the polls' demographics and the CPS figures, however, are not something to worry about. All the major media polls weight their demographic figures so that they align with the CPS figures. This type of weighting is designed to allow the underrepresented people in the survey to be accorded the same influence their group would have in the population at large, and is a standard and relatively noncontroversial method of adjustment used by most pollsters.

One worrisome result, however, was the increased underrepresentation of younger people in the rigorous survey. Instead of getting proportionately more young people by doubling the response rate, the survey got fewer—and mostly in the age group of eighteen to twenty-four. Apparently the callbacks and incentives were less effective with them.

The poll included eighty-four questions that measured respondents' attitudes and behaviors in several areas: personal trust and everyday concerns, party and ideology, political attitudes, lifestyle, and political engagement. The researchers reported that only seven individual items showed statistically significant differences between the two surveys. On the vast majority of items, the differences between the standard and rigorous surveys were negligible, with an average of only 2 percentage points per item. The inference the researchers drew from these "generally reassuring" findings was that, "within the limits of the experimental conditions," nonresponse was not such a big problem after all. Combined with the accuracy of the preelection polls in 2004, which tended to use the same procedures as Pew's standard survey, the results of the 2003 study suggested that standard polls did indeed provide valid measures of public opinion. At the very least, one of the study's implications is that it hardly makes sense for pollsters to spend the extra resources and time to contact hard-to-reach people when a standard survey produces almost the same results. That was reassuring news indeed since most media polls can't possibly take more than four months to complete if they're going to measure opinions on current subjects.

Nevertheless, there were some deeply troublesome findings about standard surveys. The 2003 Pew study found that the standard method of polling over just a few days tended to over-represent Republicans and conservatives and underrepresent moderates, compared with the hardest-to-reach respondents. The Democratic Party received a significantly lower favorable rating from the standard survey than from the rigorous survey, suggesting that, overall, Democrats may be underrepresented in most surveys compared with Republicans. The authors of the studies themselves cautioned that, with a response rate of just 50 percent in the rigorous survey, "much of the population remained beyond our view."

Robert Groves of the University of Michigan is more emphatic in cautioning people about the implications of the Pew studies, which "lead to the impression that nonresponse rates are a much smaller threat to survey estimates than suggested by prior practical guidance." Such studies need to be considered along with other research into the matter, he writes, because "in the extreme, they are misinterpreted as implying that there is rarely, if ever, a reason to worry about nonresponse bias."[10] Groves's own review of thirty articles that studied nonresponse on 335 items revealed an average of almost 9 percent difference on each item between what the poll found and what the researchers estimated would have been found if everyone in the targeted sample had been interviewed.[11] Moreover, he discovered that having high or low response rates didn't seem to affect the size of the difference or the bias in polls. Thus, he concluded, "blind pursuit of high response rates in probability samples is unwise."[12]

Groves's findings mean that media pollsters are left in a state of limbo. They have low response rates, and know that if they try to increase them, they are just as likely to cause bias as to reduce it. They also know that at least in two Pew studies, hard-to-reach respondents are not much different from those who are more willing to be interviewed, except in their partisan orientation—not a large amount, but certainly large enough to affect some results. And that's troubling, because much public policy polling and all preelection polling rely on getting accurate numbers of Republicans, Democrats, and independents in their samples.

THE PROBLEM OF nonresponse lurks in the shadow of every poll, though media pollsters would rather accept the reassuring findings of the Pew studies than contemplate the potential disaster that nonresponse could bring to the polling enterprise. Schuman was particularly critical of media polls when he wrote to the American Association for Public Opinion Research shortly after the New Hampshire primary:

> Nowadays overt and covert refusals are massive, and polling directors blithely assume that they are random or at least can be readily "adjusted for." Apparently that often works out to be the case. But it's not inevitable, and there is no license from Heaven that makes it so. Exactly where race or some other highly sensitive issue is implicit in an election is just where we might be called to account for the *casual way in which nonresponse is accepted at present*—and of course *not seriously acknowledged by even what we think of as the best polls.*[13]

As it turns out, the likelihood that the polling errors in the New Hampshire primary were caused by nonresponse is small. One theory involving racial attitudes was that pollsters were not reaching racist Democrats who were more likely to vote for a white candidate than a black one,[14] while an alternative conjecture was that white voters were unwilling to tell black interviewers they would not vote for Obama. Andrew Smith at the

Survey Center at the University of New Hampshire reported that he had checked his polling data and found no differences in reported voter preferences by race of interviewer.

In my estimation, the main reason the polls were wrong is that they stopped too early. A last-minute television news blitz on Sunday and Monday, too late to be picked up by the polls, showed an emotional Clinton coming close to tears and looking both vulnerable and strong as she explained why she was campaigning so hard for president. Another video clip shown repeatedly in the last forty-eight hours before the election was former president Bill Clinton's passionate speech that Obama's claim to wiser judgment on the Iraq war was a "fairy tale," an argument that could have relieved doubts among antiwar voters concerned about Hillary Clinton's vote in favor of war. The frequent broadcasts of these two videos during the final hours leading up the primary almost certainly influenced New Hampshire voters. And polling shows just who among those voters were most heavily influenced. Two days before the primary, the last Granite State poll showed only 34 percent of Democratic women intending to vote for Clinton. Postprimary exit polls, however, revealed that 46 percent of women wound up voting for her.

Though nonresponse was almost certainly not a major factor in the New Hampshire Democratic primary miscalls, it represents an ever-present threat to the validity of all polls. And there's not much pollsters can do about it.

Reaching Cell Phone Users

Related to the nonresponse issue is the steep increase in the number of Americans, especially young people, who rely on cell phones, which have typically been excluded from the samples used in most media polls. The cell phone issue burst into politics as a major issue for pollsters during the 2004 presidential election, when advocates for John Kerry claimed his support was underestimated by polls that had not been able to reach youthful voters. After the election, however, Pew's Scott Keeter analyzed the exit polls and concluded that while 7 percent of all voters were reachable by cell phone only, including a much higher percentage among young voters, that did not mean that the regular telephone preelection polls underestimated Kerry's vote. Polls that weighted their results to account for the under-representation of young voters generally were able to compensate for the lack of young voters with cell phones.[15] Apparently, there were few differences in attitudes between young voters who could be reached only by cell phones and those who could be reached by landline. At least for the time being, telephone polls could continue without fear of a youth bias.

It's useful to recall that general telephone surveys are a relatively recent phenomenon. From the mid-1930s through the late 1970s, most polls were conducted in respondents' homes. It was only in the late 1970s that household telephone coverage exceeded 90 percent,[16] thus allowing pollsters to switch to interviewing over the telephone. By the mid-1980s, most media polling was conducted by phone, though several important government surveys, even today, continue to interview respondents in their homes. One of these, the National Health Interview Survey,[17] collects data on the use of telephones, including cell phones. The survey itself is designed to track the health status of Americans, with the questions about phones included for subsequent contact if needed. It includes interviews with close to three thousand adults every month in all fifty states and the District of Columbia, and has a response rate of about 90 percent, providing perhaps the most accurate estimates of cell phone use in the country.

The health survey's estimates in the first half of 2007 showed that in the previous three years, the number of adults with cell phones and no home landline phone had almost tripled, from a little more than 4 percent to almost 13 percent. The potential lack of coverage was even more dramatic among young adults. Of those under age thirty, 29 percent had only a cell phone, a figure that was projected to reach 40 percent by the end of 2009.[18] It would seem that pollsters could no longer afford to exclude cell phones from their samples if they wanted to accurately represent the views of younger people.

In a special issue of *Public Opinion Quarterly* published at the end of 2007, various researchers arrived at very different conclusions about the need for pollsters to include cell phones in their samples. Pew researchers reported on four separate surveys conducted in 2006 to compare the views of cell-phone-only respondents with those of landline-phone respondents, and found that excluding cell phones did not bias poll results for *the population as a whole.* However, the authors cautioned that some results as they applied exclusively to young adults were biased because of the cell-phone exclusion. Young people with landlines are more likely to attend church and less likely to drink alcohol or approve of smoking marijuana, for example, than are young people with cell phones only. Still, the authors of the study concluded that overall, the utility of including cell-phone samples with the regular landline samples "appears marginal, at least at present."[19]

Two other teams of researchers reached quite a different conclusion, and both argued that overall results applying to the general population would be biased if cell phones are excluded. These teams used health-related data from the Centers for Disease Control, one team focusing on the national level, the other on three states. And they both concluded that the normal practice of adjusting the figures for the missing young people in landline samples no longer works. Not only are there biased figures for young people but for the population as a whole. At least when it comes to health matters—such as binge drinking, smoking, HIV testing, and having health insurance—there are significant differences between people across different ages who use only cell phones and those who can be called by landline phones.[20]

The reason for this extended debate is that interviewing respondents by cell phones poses special problems, not the least of which is increased cost to both the polling organizations and to the respondents. Unlike many countries in Europe, and unlike the protocol for landline phones in the United States, the person being called shares the cost of the connection. That could make potential respondents even more reluctant to be interviewed than people on landline phones, where refusal rates are already high. Some pollsters who have experimented with cell phones have included monetary incentives to help defray the cost to the recipient, which adds to the cost of the interview.

Even if cell phone users are willing to be interviewed, there are questions about the timing of calls, as well as where people are when they pick up the phone. With landline phones, pollsters can be reasonably assured the respondents are safely in their homes, not driving a car or engaged in some other activity that requires their full attention for safety purposes. But cell phone users seem quite willing to talk while they are driving, despite laws in many states forbidding such behavior, or to walk inattentively across a busy street while chatting on their cells. Pollsters are concerned about both the legal and ethical ramifications if their calls result in physical injury to a respondent. And then there is the timing. When it comes to cell phones, the area codes don't indicate where respondents are located when they receive the calls. They could have moved across country or be on a trip and thus be disturbed at odd moments—very late at night or early in the morning.

There are additional costs to the polling organization that are also of some concern. Federal law prohibits calling any cell phone by the use of an automatic dialer, even if a live human being is on the line when the person being called answers the phone. Many major polling organizations currently use computers to select and dial the numbers, and forgoing that efficient method would increase the cost of the surveys. Buying

special samples of cell phone numbers from sampling companies, like Survey Sampling International, would also increase
the cost to pollsters. Higher refusal rates, longer time on the
phones to go through a special set of screening questions, and
possible monetary incentives all add to the cost.

Pollsters have to evaluate all of these considerations as they
decide whether to possibly intrude into the lives of cell-phone
users in a way, place, and time that could negatively affect the
recipient. If Pew researchers are correct that including cell
phones is not necessary—at least "not as yet"—to get a representative sample, then why not wait until it becomes necessary?
"Why not indeed!" is the apparent response of most media polls
thus far. All except one.

On January 14, 2008, Frank Newport of the Gallup Poll announced that as of the beginning of the year, Gallup had added
"cell phone interviewing as part of the sample for general
population studies."[21] He admitted that it was a "complex and
costly modification in methodology," and that Gallup was making the change despite the fact that "study after study has
shown that in general, the effect of excluding from the interview process those who only have cell phones has not seemed
to affect the overall marginal results of political studies." So,
why did Gallup make such a bold change? Newport didn't say.
Mark Blumenthal, founder of pollster.com, however, suggested
that the real significance of the change was "symbolic." And
because Gallup is the "granddaddy" of the polling industry, Blumenthal expected the change to have a "big ripple effect on the
polling industry."[22]

Jim Norman, the USA Today polling representative who
works closely with Gallup in designing the questionnaires for
the USA Today/Gallup poll, sent the five screening questions
that Gallup uses for cell-phone users to pollster.com. They include asking whether the person is driving and, if so, setting a
time to call back. They also ensure that the cell phone respondent does not also have a landline phone, and that the number

is not used primarily for business purposes. The questions do not include asking what time the person is being interviewed, the assumption being that if the person answered, he or she is apparently willing to talk regardless of the hour. Nor does the protocol provide for any incentives to help pay for the connection. Although Gallup experimented with truncated interviews, they were deemed unnecessary since cell-phone respondents didn't seem any more bothered by an eighteen-minute survey than by a nine-minute one. (Gallup's maximum survey length is eighteen minutes as a matter of policy, to prevent interviewer and respondent fatigue.) As Blumenthal said of the Gallup initiative, "At the very least, this most closely watched poll will provide a regular source of data on the potential impact of the cell-phone-only households that will be missing from other surveys."[23] It's only a matter of time before the other polling organizations will follow Gallup's lead.

Internet Polling—A Dubious Alternative

As the Internet expanded into American society, Web-based surveys began to appear. Initially they were conducted mostly among special groups who already had 100 percent access to the Internet, such as college students. The surveys proved to have several advantages over telephone surveys. They can be conducted very quickly and with relatively little expense. Respondents can fill out the questionnaires at their own pace and convenience. Questions can be more elaborate, and pictures or graphs can be included where appropriate. But Internet surveys of the general public are more problematic.

Few media pollsters today believe that it's possible to obtain good national samples of adults for Internet interviewing. A major problem is that surveying over the Internet would exclude a large proportion of Americans from even being considered. To get timely responses to surveys, polling organizations would need potential respondents to access their email at least on a weekly basis, if not more frequently. Preferably, potential respondents would look at their email every day. Yet a December 2007 Pew poll found a third of all Americans saying they never use the Internet for e-mail, and nonuse goes up with age. Eventually, of course, daily Internet usage will likely become the norm for the vast majority of Americans. Regardless of usage, however, the bigger problem is that pollsters are still not able to generate a representative sample of all e-mail addresses in the country. To do that, they would need a master list of e-mail addresses from which they could draw a random sample. But no such list exists. For a sample of telephone numbers, by contrast, the master list consists of all the possible area codes, with all the possible exchanges, and all the four-digit trunk numbers. In principle, a computer can generate a random set of 10-digit telephone numbers to account for all the possible landline and cell phones in the country. In practice, there are known telephone numbers assigned to businesses, plus known blocks of unassigned numbers, which can be used to trim a computer-generated sample and make it more efficient for calling residential homes.

There is no comparable master list of e-mail addresses. The names both before and after the @ are potentially infinite in variety, with no equivalent of a numerical sequence to span the possible combinations of numbers and letters people use for their e-mail addresses. Thus, there is no practical way for a computer to generate a random set of e-mail addresses that would have any hope of covering the full range of e-mail addresses that exist in the country. And no polling organization has ever claimed to make such an effort.

The lack of sufficient Internet penetration and the inability to draw a random sample of e-mails haven't prevented at least two prominent polling organizations from claiming that they can conduct valid national public opinion surveys using the Internet: Harris Interactive, the old Louis Harris and Associates polling firm that now uses both telephones and the Internet for its polls; and Zogby International, the firm founded by John Zogby in 1984. Harris Interactive has polled for CNN, among other media outlets, while Zogby has polled mostly for Reuters, and in the 2008 presidential campaign often included CSPAN as an additional partner. When Zogby and Harris Interactive conduct polls for the media, however, they do so by telephone rather than by Internet. Still, each of the two firms conducts Internet polls during presidential elections in order to demonstrate to a skeptical audience that their Internet predictions of election winners are as good as any telephone poll.

The firms get e-mail addresses by soliciting people online to join in a "panel" of potential respondents. Harris offers rewards to potential respondents, Zogby doesn't. Anyone can sign up, and—though it's not what the firms want—can do so multiple times if they submit different identities. Once people join, they are periodically sent a survey to fill out. The more they fill out at Harris, the more rewards they get. At Zogby, the thrill of being part of a national panel is considered sufficient reward.

Harris and Zogby readily admit that the individuals thus enticed to join the firms' respective panels are not representative of Americans across the country. Online panels tend to be disproportionately white, male, young, better educated, techno-oriented, and, apparently, conservative. That last characteristic, at least, was the problem that Zogby found in 2002, and so he sought to get more liberals to balance his panel. Coincidentally, Rob Kampia of the Marijuana Policy Project had a complementary problem—he wanted more research on what Americans thought about legalizing pot for medicinal and other purposes. As Rich Morin of the *Washington Post* recounted, "Both problems went up in smoke recently when Zogby's polling firm approached Kampia's Marijuana Policy Project with a novel proposition: Help us recruit smokers and their pals to participate in our cyber-surveys, and we'll let you add a few dope questions to our national polls."[24] This was a match made in heaven. Kampia readily accepted the offer, and Zogby wound up with twelve thousand names of pot-smoking potential respondents as part of his national panel.

This is only one example of how Zogby and Harris make extraordinary efforts to recruit as large a panel of respondents as possible, regardless of how closely that final group comes to representing the American population. For each individual survey, they select a sample of their unrepresentative panel respondents, and then weight their demographic characteristics to make the sample look like the American public as described by U.S. census data with respect to such characteristics as age, gender, and region of the country. Harris adds a propensity score, which measures how frequently various groups of people use the Internet. Since, traditionally, relatively few people over the age of sixty-five have e-mail, for example, those who are included in the sample would presumably be weighted especially strongly so that their age group would be proportionate to what the U.S. Census Bureau statistics show.

To correct for misrepresentation of the public as a whole, Harris and Zogby have to rely completely on their weighting procedures, and many pollsters are skeptical that the corrective measures produce valid results. "I could run up and down K Street and select a lot of people and collect their opinions and statistically manipulate that sample to look like the United States in terms of race, sex, income, and education," Pew's Andrew Kohut told Rich Morin. "But in the end, it would still be a sample of K Street and the people would still reflect a different set of views from the country as a whole. It doesn't work."[25]

A special study by two researchers in 2005 who compared results of Web-based and telephone surveys lends credence to Kohut's comments. Overall, respondents in Harris Interactive's sample of respondents tended to be more informed, opinionated, and politically conservative than the respondents in a comparable telephone survey, even after Harris Interactive had applied its weights to compensate for their unrepresentative samples.[26]

Harris and Zogby dismiss the theoretical criticisms and implore skeptics to look at their firms' respective records in predicting elections. In doing so, however, one may not be especially reassured. In 2006, the "numbers guy" at the *Wall Street Journal*, Carl Bialik, analyzed the performance of several polling organizations that conducted numerous polls in U.S. Senate and gubernatorial races across the country. He examined the margin of victory of the winning candidate over the second place candidate as reported officially, and by the polls. The worst performance was by Zogby's Internet surveys, which had an average error of close to 9 points, twice the average of the other four polling organizations that Bialik examined. Zogby did much better with his telephone polls, which had an average error of a little more than 4 points. In the senatorial contests, "Zogby predicted a nine-point win for Democrat Herb Kohl in Wisconsin; he won by 37 points," Bialik wrote. "Democrat Maria Cantwell was expected to win by four points in Washington; she won by 17."[27] In the gubernatorial races, Zogby's average error of a little more than 8 percent was also twice as much as the telephone polling organizations Bialik studied. In six of the races, Zogby's margin of victory was off by more than 15 points.

In the 2004 presidential election, Harris Interactive produced two final estimates of the winner—the telephone poll showed Bush winning by 2 percentage points, the Internet survey showed Kerry winning by 3.[28] Clearly, the telephone poll was the better predictor, and it mirrored most of the other telephone preelection polls. Harris Interactive also conducted Web-based surveys on the presidential contest in three states: Florida, Ohio, and Pennsylvania. In Florida, the average error among eleven telephone polls was 5 points, whereas Harris Interactive was off by 9 points. In Ohio, the average error among ten telephone polls was 1.9 points; Harris Interactive was off by 6. In Pennsylvania, Harris Interactive's error was just 1 point, while the average of seven telephone polls was 1.9 points. These results suggest that, overall, telephone polls continue to do a better job of predicting election outcomes.

In the long run, it seems doubtful that Internet surveys like those conducted by Zogby and Harris Interactive will replace telephone surveys for most media polls. The problem is that the foundation of science is transparency—the methods of investigation have to be clearly visible for all to see, so that other researchers, following the same methods, can presumably arrive at the same results. But the methods of Harris Interactive and Zogby are secret. The propensity score that Harris Interactive applies to its Web-based surveys, apparently derived from data the firm gets from its phone surveys, is something it will not disclose. It is Harris's special recipe, which magically produces plausible results, and we are allowed only to judge the performance record—not the process. Zogby is equally secretive about the way he selects respondents from his panel for any given survey and then weights his data to force his samples into line with the U.S. census. What is known about the two firms' methods is that they violate many of the scientific approaches developed over the past several decades for obtaining representative samples of the general public. Until there is more transparency, it probably doesn't matter to most pollsters that Harris and Zogby can sometimes predict election outcomes within a small margin of error; after all, one of the most successful presidential polls ever taken was the *Literary Digest*'s 1932 poll, despite severely flawed sampling and data collection methods. There's no assurance that the inherently flawed approach of the Internet polls won't suffer a similar fate.

ONE WEB-BASED polling organization has not abandoned the principles of scientific sampling and transparency of its survey methods. Founded in 1998 by two Stanford University professors, Knowledge Networks recruits its panel members by using standard U.S. telephone probability samples to initially call respondents and ask them if they would be willing to participate in the firm's Internet surveys. For households that do not have Internet access, the firm provides them the hardware and a connection for free. As the firm notes on its website, "Short of in-person ('door to door') recruitment, this is the only way to recruit a probability based panel and is the only way to create a projectable, representative on-line sample."[29]

This approach is quite expensive, of course. The firm says online that it has about forty-three thousand active panelists and that the maximum number of respondents nationwide that it is likely to get (if it sent e-mail solicitations to all panelists at one time) is about thirty thousand, a sizable number given that most media polls have national samples of about a thousand to fifteen hundred respondents. Of course, Knowledge Networks wouldn't typically send questionnaires to all its panelists for a single national survey, but would instead select a subset from that larger group. Still, the firm's panel size is far smaller than what Zogby and Harris Interactive claim to have. The compelling advantage of the Knowledge Networks panel is that it has been selected using scientific criteria. "Professional panelists"—people who seek out Internet companies to win rewards by filling out surveys—are not a problem for Knowledge Networks, though they are for Harris Interactive. Thus the bias injected by self-selected respondents, which is inherent in the Harris Interactive and Zogby panels, is eliminated by the Knowledge Networks sampling process.

Not all is rosy for Knowledge Networks, though. The response rate of the initial telephone samples is quite low, lower than the response rates for normal telephone polls, because of the added commitment of participating in periodic surveys. For people who don't have access to the Internet already, or don't have e-mail, the response rate is particularly low, because joining the firm's panel requires a change from their normal behavior. And like other telephone polls, Knowledge Networks faces the challenge of cell-phone-only users. The firm can't even re-cruit such people unless it moves to include cell phones as part of its initial sampling frame. Yet, for all of these problems, Knowledge Networks is leading the way into Internet polling that does not abandon the principles of scientific sampling.

The More Things Change . . .

While the polling industry continues to adjust to changing tech-nologies, none of the problems discussed here suggests that public opinion polling will go away. It's clear that increasing nonresponse is a serious challenge to the validity of polls, but current research suggests that the bias caused by people choos-ing not to participate in polls is not a death knell. Apart from nonresponse, the spread of cell-phone use is only a minor in-convenience so far, an additional operating expense but not an insurmountable obstacle to measuring the will of the public. Scientific, Web-based surveys can be done now, but the best current approach is prohibitively expensive. Once the Internet has reached close to 90 percent penetration, pollsters might fol-low Knowledge Networks' lead and use telephone samples (in-cluding cell phones) to acquire representative samples of e-mail addresses. By then, cell phones may be so widespread that they will be the principal method by which pollsters regularly con-nect with respondents—either directly with interviewers, as is the case now, or with Internet connections directly to the cell phones. Perhaps even in the next decade or so, some scientific surveys of public opinion might well be conducted through the use of text messages.

Yet none of these technological changes will substantially affect the underlying problems with today's media polls. Unless changes are made in the way questions are asked and responses are analyzed, media polls will still manufacture public opinion. They will continue to serve the interests of the powerful at the expense of the public. And they will cause more and more peo-ple in that public, as well as an increasing number of political observers, to denounce polls as a blight on democracy rather than appreciate them for the real contribution they can, and should, make to our democratic process.

CHAPTER EIGHT

A New Direction

The power of polls today far exceeds the visions of the early pollsters, who simply hoped that their scientific measurements of the public will would enhance the democratic process. But as I've made clear, that power is not always positive. The problem is that media polls today are designed to conceal the truth about the American public, a truth that everybody knows but that journalists and pollsters are reluctant to acknowledge.

Virtually everyone who studies or measures public opinion today recognizes that there is a distinction between what Daniel Katz called "a superficially held view which may be discarded the next moment" and "a cherished conviction which will change only under unusual pressure."[1] The current academic debate focuses mostly on how to differentiate between the two extremes. Some researchers suggest there is a spectrum, from non-attitudes to quasi-attitudes to real attitudes. Quasi-attitudes are in the middle of the spectrum, because they signify lightly held views that tend to correlate with other opinions and demographic characteristics but also tend to be quite "labile."[2] The issue is where along this spectrum it makes sense to draw the line between opinion and non-opinion.

However unresolved the debate may be among academics,

among pollsters there is a standard format that roughly gets at non-opinions for policy preferences. After asking whether respondents favor or oppose a policy, pollsters can add a tag line: "Or are you unsure?"[3] There are other similar formulations, such as "Or don't you know enough to say?" and "Or haven't you given this enough thought?" Another frequently used tactic is to ask respondents how much they have heard about an issue. Those who have not heard anything are sometimes assumed not to have an opinion, so the policy question is not asked of them. That was the approach the Gallup Poll often used before it was bought out by SRI and became a media partner with CNN and *USA Today.* Pew Research and several other media polls still employ that method, though not for all policy questions.

Despite the ease of measuring non-opinion, pollsters rarely do it because the media don't usually find it newsworthy. That's why it was remarkable in late October 2007 that Gallup reported the results of its most recent poll, which stressed how little Americans knew about the economic sanctions the United States had just imposed on Iran.[4] Gallup's question on the issue began pretty typically, feeding respondents information: "As you may know, Secretary of State Condoleezza Rice announced Thursday that the United States was imposing economic sanctions against two agencies of the Iranian government and three Iranian banks." But this time, for no apparent reason, Gallup deviated from the forced-choice format so often used in public policy polls, and decided to allow respondents to admit they didn't have an opinion. "From what you know or have read," the question asked, "do you favor or oppose these sanctions—or don't you know enough to say?" More than half of the respondents, 57 percent, opted for the latter choice, while 34 percent said they favored, and 9 percent said they opposed the sanctions. There was no follow-up question to measure intensity of opinion, but at least the poll revealed the fact that many people had no opinion at all.

Gallup's willingness to measure public ignorance on the sanctions surprised me, and I wrote to Frank Newport praising the approach (I had made my preference for that format clear during the years I worked at Gallup). I also asked what had prompted the action and whether it signaled a change in policy. He responded that there hadn't been a change in policy since I had left the year before. The decision to measure non-opinion in this case was made because Secretary Rice had just announced the sanctions a couple of days earlier, and they were quite complicated.[5] That, of course, is an eminently reasonable explanation, which essentially recognizes how few people would know anything about such a complex issue.

The sad truth is that on many, if not most, other issues, public ignorance is just as substantial—though it usually goes unmeasured. Gallup's policy on measuring non-opinion in the years that I worked there was essentially no policy at all. In the rare case that our media partners thought the issue might best be framed as one where public ignorance was the story, we would measure non-opinion accordingly. It was strictly an ad hoc, arbitrary choice. Otherwise, we stuck to the tried-and-true forced-choice questions, as do the other media polls generally. I've talked with pollsters at other media polling organizations, and they too indicated that they decide on a case-by-case basis when to measure non-opinion. The problem is that it doesn't make sense for pollsters to say that in one instance it's important to tell the truth about what the public doesn't know, but in other cases it's not. That's a deliberately manipulative tactic that cannot help but undercut pollsters' claims of scientific objectivity.

To tell the truth about Americans' opinions on policy matters, pollsters should routinely measure the extent of public ignorance. It will never be zero, and in most cases it will represent a substantial proportion of the citizenry. Measuring it costs nothing; all it requires is offering an option that allows respondents to admit that they don't have an opinion. Because it's an important element in understanding the public, suppressing it for commercial or other purposes is simply unacceptable.

In addition, pollsters should include at least one additional question to measure the intensity of respondents' opinions. I would prefer a measure along the lines suggested earlier in this book, asking respondents if they would be "upset" if their opinion were not followed. There are other approaches, such as asking whether the issue is important to the respondents, or whether it would affect their vote for a political candidate. Whatever the approach, it's important to distinguish between the lightly held, top-of-mind response, which can change in an instant, and the more deeply held opinions that respondents want to see prevail.

Finally, pollsters should stop giving crash tutorials to respondents about situations or proposals. Once respondents have been fed any information, they no longer represent the general public. Noted Democratic campaign pollster Peter Hart, who also co-conducts the NBC/*Wall Street Journal* poll, argues that giving respondents information before asking them questions gives pollsters a good insight into what people *might* think if they were informed about an issue.[6] I disagree with the tactic, because the general public will almost never be "informed" about an issue the same way the respondents are, so the informed sample will never represent the uninformed general public, even on a hypothetical basis. On the other had, *if* pollsters insist on feeding information, at the very least they should openly admit that their results are speculative, rather than treat them as though they represent what the general public is actually thinking today. Unfortunately, pollsters who adopt this tactic almost never reveal the hypothetical nature of their results.

Any description of the general public's orientation toward specific policy proposals needs to mention explicitly how large is the size of the disengaged public—the proportion of people who admit up front that they have no opinion, plus those who initially express a view but immediately say that they don't care if it is ignored by elected leaders. Anytime a poll reports less that 20 percent of the public disengaged, it's almost certain the results have been manipulated and should be viewed with deep suspicion.

WHILE IT'S EASIER to assess when election polls are right and wrong, in truth they're just as twisted by manipulation as surveys on public policy. Media pollsters have become so used to it that they either don't see the problem, or they recognize it but can't bring themselves to break from the pack. It may be impossible, for example, to wean pollsters and pundits off their addiction to the nonexistent national primary electorate. Pollsters like it because it's so easy to poll Democrats and Republicans nationally, and to pretend that the results really mean something.

After Super Tuesday in 2008, the focus for Democrats rightly shifted to how many delegates each candidate had won —since the number of delegates determines who becomes the party's presidential nominee. Yet right before those elections, USA Today's Susan Page reported on the latest USA Today/ Gallup poll of the fictitious national primary electorate, which found "a Democratic race between Barack Obama and Hillary Rodham Clinton that remains too close to call."[7] The statement was deeply flawed. That "race" she mentioned was no race at all, and it would never be "called," because the Democratic nomination would not be decided by a public opinion contest among Democrats nationally. But she had Gallup's "Daily Tracking" data and wanted her newspaper to say *something* about the nomination contest. It's better, apparently, to report something irrelevant than to report nothing at all.

Such thinking was also at play when ABC posted its latest national primary poll before Super Tuesday on February 3,

2008. The headlines read: "POLL: A Tight Fight for Clinton/ Obama While McCain Extends His Surge."[8] The article that followed began, "Days before nearly half the country votes in the Super Tuesday primaries, Hillary Clinton and Barack Obama are locked in a tight race for the Democratic presidential nomination," giving readers the distinct impression that the "tight race" referred to in the article was in the Super Tuesday states, where people would vote. Not so. This article and its poll numbers referred to the tight race among Democrats and Republicans nationally, the vast majority of whom would not be voting on Super Tuesday. I e-mailed ABC's Gary Langer, asking him why he didn't screen the results from his national samples to look at just the Super Tuesday states. At least potentially, those might be *real* voters. He wrote back to say:

> We could pull out just those states (and did look at them informally). But to be most meaningful it would require screening to match each state's voting rules—open, partially closed, closed— and much more assiduous [likely voter] modeling, even with different models for different states. Pretty complicated, and honestly simply not our aim. We're looking to see where the country's at, not to predict how the 24 states will go.[9]

Langer's response is an unusually candid admission that gets at the heart of why pollsters like the fictitious national primaries: they're easy. The fact that the *country* doesn't vote together and all at once is just an inconvenient detail. By taking an inaccurate and misleading macro view, pollsters can avoid the "much more assiduous" efforts required for polling in primary states.

In fact, most of the major media polls do not poll extensively in caucus and primary states, leaving that task to various local and commercial polling organizations looking for publicity. When the major media polls do conduct surveys in selected state contests, they typically do so long before the election so they can avoid having their final results compared with the actual vote, a comparison that could possibly hurt their reputations. In New Hampshire, it was unusual that CBS, CNN, and *USA Today*/Gallup had all polled close enough to Election Day to make predictions of the outcome. After that debacle, all of the major media polls recognized the danger and in subsequent states avoided tempting fate. The *New York Times* polling editor, Janet Elder, was surprisingly frank in admitting her newspaper's decision to avoid polling immediately before primaries. "We don't want to appear to be projecting results," she said. "We've learned that opinion is in such flux in the last days before people vote that we tend to stand back."[10] Mostly, the major media polls spent their resources and time on the irrelevant, but less challenging, national primary electorate so they could at least pretend they had important insights to contribute to unfolding events.

USA Today and ABC and the *New York Times,* along with all the other major media pollsters, are in good company. It was George Gallup who started the national primary polling, because he, too, wanted to avoid polling in actual state primaries and caucus states, where opinion was too unsettled to measure accurately. As Alec Gallup acknowledged in a recent interview, when his father began polling Republicans and Democrats nationally, he did so "knowing it didn't have a lot to do with the real world. It was something to do"—to provide his subscribers some public opinion information.[11] At that time, of course, party conventions chose presidential candidates, and the few primary elections that were held served mostly as "beauty contests," giving candidates an opportunity to demonstrate their electoral appeal. In the 1970s, the political parties handed over power to the voters to select delegates to the national nominating conventions. That shift in power from party leaders to the rank-and-file party members transformed the way presidential candidates are nominated. Now the news media and polls dominate the nomination process, and people pay attention to what the polls say. Unfortunately, what was mostly a sales gimmick when Gallup started the tradition of polling Democrats and Republicans nationally has become, in this new political environment, a hallowed institution that too many people accept as real. Pretending that a national electorate exists is no longer just a harmless gimmick, but a real detriment to the democratic process.

APART FROM BEATING the fictitious national primary electorate into the ground and burying it under a block of concrete, pollsters can improve preelection polling by always measuring and reporting the percentage of undecided voters. Not to do so misrepresents the electorate, which can in turn exert a profound effect on election campaigns, from fund-raising to recruiting volunteers. Measuring the undecided vote would not require pollsters to give up their cherished vote choice question, "Who would you vote for if the election were held today?" It does mean that a separate question is needed to measure how committed voters are to the candidates. The approach adopted by the University of New Hampshire Survey Center for CNN, WMUR-TV, and separately for the *Boston Globe,* worked well. The important contribution that it made—by asking, at the beginning of the interview, whether a voter had definitely decided, was leaning, or had not yet decided whom to vote for—was to disabuse its readers and viewers of the prevailing conventional wisdom that one of the candidates had the election locked up. It gave a realistic picture of the primary contest in New Hampshire and avoided the mistake that others made in the fall of 2007 in treating Clinton's supposed double-digit lead as though it were insurmountable. It continually showed a large percentage of undecided Republican voters, which also helped explain why John McCain was able to come back from being low in the "national primary" polls to win in New Hampshire.

At the end of the campaign, when pollsters feel obligated to make final predictions, it's possible to press voters on their candidate preferences without hurting the electoral process. Pollsters at that time are no longer trying to find out what the *current* state of the electorate is, but are trying to predict what it will be one or two days hence. The only thing at stake is their reputations, with the final predictions—whether precise or not —unlikely to affect the campaigns. The last CNN/WMUR-TV/ UNH Survey Center poll did in fact press respondents for their preferences, and its final predictions on the Republican side were as accurate as any, while its final predictions on the Democratic race suffered the same fate as the other polls. The redeeming aspect of the poll on the Democratic primary was that it alerted readers up front that a substantial proportion of the Democratic electorate was still undecided—27 percent were leaning toward a candidate, and 21 percent more were still trying to decide.

When pollsters pressure undecided voters to say who they will vote for if the election were held "today," they are really trying to find out who those voters will support on *Election Day.* "Today," the undecided voters have already told us, they are unsure—*that* is what they are thinking at the time of the poll. It's pollsters who believe that if they force respondents to pretend the election is being held right now, voters will offer a response that they will abide by later. But these undecided voters don't care what they tell pollsters under duress. That's what Frank Newport meant when he explained, perhaps tongue in cheek, why the 2008 New Hampshire Democratic Primary polls were wrong. "My best hypothesis is that Democratic voters in New Hampshire *didn't cooperate with pollsters* by maintaining their weekend voting intentions," he wrote on *USA Today* online, "but instead continued to evaluate candidates and to take new information into account right up until the time they went into the voting booth."[12] Shame on voters for not cooperating with pollsters! But woe to those pollsters who reported only 2 percent undecided.[13]

Fuzzy Opinion

Pollsters have known for a long time that election and public policy polls alike produce, at best, rough estimates of what the public is thinking. From the beginning of modern polling, experiments have shown that even small differences in question wording, or the order in which questions are read, can have a profound effect on results. The gender and race of interviewers, as well as whether surveys are conducted by telephone or online, through the mail, or in person can also affect responses. George Gallup was the first to conduct experiments that revealed the fuzziness of opinion, but he maintained a belief that the right questions, objectively worded, could accurately measure the will of the people. His vision was that polls would be able to continuously monitor "the pulse of democracy." It turns out that on most issues the public's pulse is either a bit weak or harder to discern than Gallup had hoped.

When it comes to question wording, experiments have shown that the public is more likely to favor a policy when the government will "not allow" some behavior than when it will "forbid" that same behavior. There is much more public support for programs described as "assistance to the poor" than those labeled "welfare." Proposals that are linked to salient politicians or institutions will usually generate different levels of support than when the proposals are evaluated without such association. These days, any question that suggests a policy is supported by a political party or by the president will immediately trigger partisan responses, almost regardless of substance.

So influential is the way a question is framed, the political lexicon is undergoing continual transformation as proponents and opponents of various policies vie for the most appealing wording. "Partial-birth abortion" versus "late-term abortion," the "estate tax" versus the "death tax," "pro-choice" versus "pro-life," and "abuse of prisoners" versus "torture" are just a few examples. Pollsters will often find themselves besieged by various interest groups who disagree with the way a question may be worded, because they see it as biased and possibly detrimental to their cause. And with good reason—the very language of opinion polls can influence how people respond.

One prime example of the complexity of the wording issue, and its implications, is the ongoing controversy over how to address the public's view of homosexuality. For many years, various gay and lesbian activists have objected to the Gallup question, "Do you feel that homosexuality should be considered an acceptable alternative lifestyle or not?" Their most trenchant objection is to the phrasing, "alternative lifestyle," implying that homosexuality is a choice, and a frivolous one at that. No one would think of "straight" people as having a "heterosexual lifestyle." And it doesn't help that "alternative lifestyle" was the jargon often used to refer to hippies of the 1960s who would "drop out" of the mainstream culture. To talk about gays and lesbians in that terminology today has become unacceptable.

In 1996 and again in 1999,[14] Gallup used a split-sample experiment to test new wording, asking half the respondents in the sample the standard question and the other half, "Do you feel that homosexual behavior should be considered an acceptable lifestyle or not?" This version substituted "homosexual behavior" for "homosexuality," and it got rid of "alternative." There were no significant differences in the results based on the two questions, suggesting that the wording changes made little difference to the general public. Still, the new wording hardly satisfied the critics, especially because the word "lifestyle" was still included.

In 1997, Gallup tested the standard question against another version, again using the split-sample experiment—asking half the sample the old question, and the other half the new question: "Do you feel that homosexuality should be considered acceptable, or not?"[15] Gone from the new version was the controversial wording "alternative lifestyle." It produced the same results as the standard question, which meant that it could be substituted for the old wording without affecting the trend. Frank Newport decided, however, to keep the old wording. Because public opinion didn't seem to be affected by the description that gays and lesbians found so offensive, he thought it was better to keep the question that had been used for seventeen years.

In 2005, again in response to critics wanting to update the terminology, and using the same split-sample experiment technique, Gallup tried out this wording: "Do you feel that gay or lesbian relations should be considered acceptable, or not?"[16] This was the most modern version Gallup had ever tried. Gone were "homosexuality" and "alternative lifestyle." To that version of the question, 60 percent of respondents said such relations were acceptable, whereas only 51 percent said that "homosexuality should be considered an acceptable alternative lifestyle." The 9-point difference forced Gallup to face a major dilemma. Higher public support for "gay or lesbian relations" suggested that respondents were negatively influenced by Gallup's standard question. The critics could now justifiably claim that Gallup was biasing the results by adhering to language that had long since passed out of favor. On the other hand, Gallup was concerned not just with the specific percentage it measured in 2005, but with the overall trend. Since 1984, it had used the standard question (though occasionally trying out a different wording on half the sample) to give a picture of how public opinion on this issue had evolved. With Gallup's data, one could see that the public had become more accepting of "homosexuality" over the years, a trend that could be confused by introducing new language; any apparent increase in support could be ascribable to the new language rather than to a real change in opinion. Gallup decided to keep the old wording.

In 2007, a Gallup article announced that polls showed "tolerance for gay rights at high water mark," based on the standard question.[17] Yet keeping the old question is not necessarily the optimum solution, according to such critics as George Bishop,[18] who take issue with the notion that just because the question is the same over time, it measures the same phenomenon. Bishop's reasoning is that words take on new meanings as the culture evolves, which is why no poll today would ask about "negroes"—though it was the enlightened term for pollsters to use during much of the twentieth century. Similarly, the words "homosexuality" and "alternative lifestyle" may have taken on more negative nuances over the past quarter century, making the trend data as problematic as any new question wording.

This example illustrates that public opinion measures can easily be affected by what some people might see as relatively slight differences in question wording. It also illustrates the dilemma that pollsters have when confronted with trends that go back many years, but which are based on flawed question wording. Changing the wording may affect the measures, suggesting changes when none has occurred. But keeping the wording may cause its own distortions.

In this case, I would have opted to keep both versions going by using the split-sample approach, asking half the sample the standard question, the other half the new question. That would have allowed Gallup to continue with the trend question for a few more years, which apparently it wanted to do, while asking the new, more relevant question as the main one to report. Still, no decision is perfect, given how problematic are all measures of public opinion.

APART FROM QUESTION WORDING, poll measures can also be influenced by the order in which two options are presented. Over the telephone, people are more likely to choose the second answer than the first one, all other things being equal. That's particularly true with long or complicated questions, when people don't really have an opinion and wind up choosing what they last heard the interviewer say. In 2005, after the disastrous federal emergency response to Hurricane Katrina, Gallup wanted to know whether Americans blamed bad planning or the bureaucracy itself. The question it asked was,

> In your view, which was the greater obstacle to the federal government's response to the hurricane?
> a. Neglecting domestic needs like emergency preparedness and infrastructure in the past, or
> b. Bureaucratic inefficiency.

Half the respondents were asked the question as just described, whereas the other half were presented first with option B, followed by option A. The original question found a 24-point majority blaming bureaucratic inefficiency over neglecting domestic needs—57 percent to 33 percent. The other version of the question, with option A presented second, found an 8-point margin citing "neglecting domestic needs" as the greater obstacle—48 percent to 40 percent. That represented a 32-point swing in public opinion, based solely on the order in which the two options were read.[19]

Other experiments show that polling results can be affected by the order in which questions are asked. During the Clinton presidency, Bill Clinton was given higher favorable ratings when he was evaluated after Al Gore than when he was rated first. Gore, on the other hand, was given lower ratings after respondents rated Clinton than when Gore was rated first. A majority of Americans approve of a woman having an abortion if she can't afford to raise the child, when that question is the first one posed about abortion. Far fewer Americans express support when that question is asked after others that suggest even more compelling reasons for an abortion, such as the mother's health and safety. People are more likely to express support for same-sex unions if they have first been asked about their support for same-sex marriage. These and other examples illustrate how difficult it is for pollsters to conduct a poll on many topics with scores of questions. The answers to questions asked several minutes into the survey may well be influenced by the questions that were asked earlier.

Interestingly, telephone poll results are sometimes influenced by the perceived race of the people asking the questions. Studies have shown that black respondents tend to give more skeptical answers about civil rights progress when they believe they are speaking to black interviewers than to white interviewers. White respondents, by contrast, tend to give more optimistic responses when they think the interviewers are black. Some observers thought that the failure of the polls to predict Hillary Clinton's victory in the 2008 New Hampshire primary was ascribable in part to the unwillingness of white Democrats to tell black interviewers they would not support Barack Obama. A similar phenomenon may have been at work in 1989, when Democrat David Dinkins was running for mayor of New York City. Polls showed him leading by a substantial margin, but his real margin of victory was narrow. Some researchers at the time suggested that white Democratic voters didn't want to tell pollsters, especially black interviewers, that they were not going to support a black candidate. As it turned out, Andrew Smith of the UNH Survey Center found no race-of-interviewers effects in New Hampshire in 2008. Still, the larger issue remains—on some issues, the opinions that pollsters measure can be affected by the perceived racial characteristics of the interviewers.

Similarly, on issues that tend to divide men and women, the interviewer's gender can affect what a respondent might say. Male respondents tend to be more supportive of equal rights for women, for example, when talking with female interviewers than with males. In a statewide survey on child abuse in the 1980s, I found that men were systematically more willing to admit to female interviewers than to male interviewers that they had severely punished their children. That seemed counterintuitive to me until my sociology colleagues explained that men are generally more open to admitting weaknesses and problems when talking with women than with men—and this tendency can be reflected in male-female interactions on the phone as well.

Studies suggest that vote choice, however, is not influenced by interviewer's gender—each candidate's support is about the same when measured by a male or female interviewer. But on such issues as whether men and women receive equal treatment or whether men's or women's lives are easier, the interviewer's gender is likely to influence what people say.

All these examples illustrate that any measure of public opinion is at best a rough approximation of what people are thinking. And the plus or minus 3 percent margin of sampling error reported by most polls is only the least of possible errors.

Fulfilling the Promise

Sixteen years ago, at the end of my book on the contemporary history of public opinion polls, *The Superpollsters*, I concluded that "Gallup's vision of polling as an instrument for improving the practice of democracy seems largely vindicated."[20] I no longer hold such an optimistic view. Instead I've come to realize, as did one of the polling giants of the past half century, Daniel Yankelovich, that "despite the polling profession's greater technical sophistication, polls have grown ever more misleading. Far from serving to give leaders insight into the real concerns of the public, they often add to the lack of confidence that disconnects the leadership class in the United States from the mainstream of the citizenry."[21]

That doesn't have to be the case. The argument today is not about developing a new conception of public opinion in which polls have little or no role. It's about having polls remain in their central role by making sure they tell the whole story about what the public is thinking—to include not just what preferences it has, but also what proportion of the public has no preferences at all. Telling the truth about public opinion gets at the heart of why opinion is central to a democratic form of government. When political scientists Lawrence Jacobs and Robert Shapiro argued, as cited in the preface to this book, that elected leaders need to respond to centrist public opinion, implicit in their argument is the assumption that polls accurately report what that opinion is. The polls do not currently fulfill that function. And for democracy's sake, they must.

This is not an argument for direct democracy, in which leaders would blindly follow, or attempt to follow, what the people say. A representative democracy requires constant interplay between leaders and citizens, with citizens providing the overall framework of values within which elected leaders have to make specific detailed decisions. Some part of the public will always be disengaged, just as some part will always be extremely knowledgeable and active in pressing their point of view. And it is helpful in the process for leaders to know the truth about their constituents' commitment to one position or another— how many genuinely want a given outcome, how many are willing to be persuaded, and how many are willing to defer judgment to their leaders. Ultimately, the choice is not an absolute division between what the people want and what politicians want. Instead, the process is more dynamic, in which leaders propose and discuss options, helping to educate people on the implications of policies, and thus shape—but not manipulate— public opinion in a direction that benefits the common interest. In turn, polls can be used to gauge the public's general reaction to different proposals, though usually not the arcane details. But polls can only be useful in this context if they measure that reaction accurately.

It's always possible that with this new approach to measuring public opinion, which explicitly reveals the extent of public disengagement, some politicians will assume they can therefore do whatever they want without fear of voter retribution. And in many cases that would be correct. There are few occasions in which so many people are actively engaged in a single issue that it can determine the outcome of an election. Most legislation goes unnoticed by the vast majority of the public, so indeed the Congress and the president can in principle "get away with" enacting many laws that serve the interests of the few at the expense of the many. But media polls cannot prevent such abuse. Nor do they enable or encourage it. Politicians who regularly disregard the public interest do that regardless of what polls say. The fear of such behavior in no way justifies the current practice of manufacturing false results to conceal public ignorance and apathy.

The real problem with telling the truth about the public and the electorate is not that the elected leaders or the public can't handle it, but that the news media might find it dull. Journalists like sharply divided groups and extreme reactions because that makes their stories more exciting. They like the fake stories about voter preferences years ahead of the election, and the exciting horse race of a fully decided electorate that nevertheless keeps changing its mind. They have become addicted to the fictitious national primary electorate, and entranced by their own illusion of a completely rational, all-knowing, and fully engaged public. Should they be forced to report on the real public, a more prosaic public of which large segments are minimally informed or disengaged or have opinions that are ambiguous or tentative, journalists might lose their obsessive fascination with polls. That could happen to some extent, though I doubt even polls that told the unvarnished truth about the public would lose their journalistic appeal completely. But even if pollsters believed that a reformed polling system would cause the news media to rely less often on poll reports, that's no argument for pollsters to continue pumping up false numbers to satisfy the press's unrealistic expectations.

I'm hopeful, if not wildly optimistic, that we are witnessing a historical phase that will soon pass, and that a more responsible approach to measuring public opinion lies in the not-too-distant future. Widespread dissatisfaction with polls can only increase as their dismal performances continue. Eventually, the many conflicting and nonsensical results should shame pollsters and the news media into reform. Only if that happens will polls achieve their ideal role in the democratic process—telling the truth about the public, warts and all.

ACKNOWLEDGMENTS

The critique in this book has been germinating for a long time, and I thank my many colleagues in the American Association for Public Opinion Research over the years who have opposed, discussed, praised, dismissed, supported, and inspired the ideas that have given shape to my arguments. The association's annual conference is an exciting intellectual and social experience that I would recommend to anyone who regularly produces, uses, or has any interest in survey research results.

I am especially grateful to Mark Crispin Miller of New York University and to W. Lance Bennett of the University of Washington for their early enthusiasm with my ideas about the problems of polling, and for their suggestions to expand the critique from a narrow focus on polls to include the media environment in which the polls have come to play such an important role.

My appreciation also to Mil Duncan and the Carsey Institute at the University of New Hampshire, which provided both logistical support for the writing and analysis, as well as a collegial review of my early efforts. Murray Straus and the Family Research Laboratory also provided both collegial and logistical support, for which I am very grateful. Thanks also to Andy Smith, the director of the University of New Hampshire Survey

Center, who helped me test ideas in questionnaire design and provided access to research data.

Special thanks to Allison Trzop, a superb editor at Beacon Press, who worked with me at every stage of the manuscript writing to produce as clear and forceful an explication of my ideas as possible. Whatever the quality of the book, it is far better than it would have been without her help. Thanks also to Jim McCarthy, my agent at Dystell & Goderich, whose early enthusiasm and constructive advice helped launch the project.

Eric, Allison, Leeyanne, and Josh invariably inspire me by their enthusiasm for all my writing efforts. And to Zelda, for her insights, support, inspiration, and understanding, I am always indebted.

NOTES

Preface: Pollsters under Attack

1. President James A. Garfield in a speech to the U.S. House of Representatives in 1869, cited in Theodore Caplow, Louis Hicks, Ben J. Wattenberg, *The First Measured Century: An Illustrated Guide to Trends in America, 1900–2000* (Washington, DC: AEI Press, 2001), p. xii.

2. Sarah E. Igo, *The Averaged American: Surveys, Citizens, and the Making of a Mass Public* (Cambridge, MA: Harvard University Press, 2007), on the book jacket.

3. Harold D. Lasswell, *Democracy through Public Opinion* (Menasha, WI: George Banta, 1941), p. 15.

4. Lawrence R. Jacobs and Robert Y. Shapiro, *Politicians Don't Pander: Political Manipulation and the Loss of Democratic Responsiveness* (Chicago: University of Chicago Press, 2000), p. 339.

5. David W. Moore, "Bush Bounce Keeps on Going: President Leads Kerry by 13 Points among Likely Voters; 8 Points among Registered Voters," Gallup website, www.gallup.com/poll/13066/Bush-Bounce-Keeps-Going .aspx#3, Sept. 17, 2004.

6. For a comparison of polls at this time, including the conflict between Gallup and Pew, see Carl Hulse, "Varying Polls Reflect Volatility, Experts Say," *New York Times*, Sept. 18, 2004.

7. Ibid.

8. "Dewey Beats Truman," editorial in the *Raleigh (NC) News and Observer*, Nov. 6, 2004, p. A22. http://nl.newsbank.com/nl-search/we/Archives? p_product=NewsLibrary&p_action=home&p_theme=newslibrary2&s_

home=home&s_sources=home&p_clear_search=&s_search_type=
keyword&s_place=&s_category=none.

9. Christopher Hitchens, "A Crushing Defeat," quoted on www
.slingsnarrows.com/blog/2004_11.html, Nov. 30, 2004.

10. Cited by Martin Plissner, "In Defense of Exit Polls: You Just Don't
Know How to Use Them," *Slate*, Nov. 4, 2004 (www.slate.com/id/2109186).

11. Jimmy Breslin, "Making Call on Sham of Political Polling," *Newsday*,
Sept. 16, 2004 (removed from website, but cited at www.theleftcoaster.com/
archives/002684.php).

12. Peter Coy, "Pollsters Score Low with the Public," *Businessweek*,
May 20, 2004 (www.businessweek.com/print/bwdaily/dnflash/may2004/nf
20040520_8555_db038.htm?chan=db).

13. Frank Rich, "Ask Not What J.F.K. Can Do for Obama," *New York
Times*, Feb. 30, 2008 (www.nytimes.com/2008/02/03/opinion/03rich.html).

14. The order in which the polling partners' names appear is flexible. Typically, each polling partner will list its own name first, though Gallup tended
to list its own name last. CNN and *USA Today* always listed their names first
and Gallup's last. That meant that "Gallup" was always followed by "poll."
Whether the order of the names had any effect on anyone's view of the
polling organization has never been tested, to my knowledge.

Chapter One: Iraq and the Polls—The Myth of War Support

1. Arianna Huffington, "The 77 Percent Solution," May 7, 2003, at
http://ariannaonline.huffingtonpost.com/columns/column.php?id=19.

2. See David W. Moore, "The New Arianna Huffington...Pro-Polls?,"
on the Gallup website, July 15, 2003 www.gallup.com/poll/8836/New-
Arianna-Huffington-ProPolls.aspx.

3. Arianna Huffington, "Partnership for a Poll-Free America," on her
website, http://ariannaonline.huffingtonpost.com/crusades/pollfree.php.

4. All public opinion results reported here come from the *Polling Report*
(www.pollingreport.com/iraq13.htm).

5. Elisabeth Noelle-Neumann, *The Spiral of Silence: Public Opinion—
Our Social Skin*, 2nd ed. (Chicago: University of Chicago Press, 1993), p. 202.

6. Among the accounts of the press's rush to support the war, see
W. Lance Bennett, Regina G. Lawrence, and Steven Livingston, *When the
Press Fails: Political Power and the News Media from Iraq to Katrina*
(Chicago: University of Chicago Press, 2007); Michael Massing, *Now They
Tell Us* (New York: New York Review of Books, 2004); and Eric Boehlert,
Lapdogs: How the Press Rolled Over for Bush (New York: Free Press, 2006).

7. See David W. Moore and Jeff Jones, "Permissive Consensus: A New Paradigm for Public Policy Research," manuscript available from either author, Dec. 5, 2007.

8. Humphrey Taylor, letter to the editor, *New York Times*, Dec. 7, 2001.

9. Anthony Lewis, "Abroad at Home, Dust in Our Eyes," *New York Times*, Dec. 4, 2001.

10. William Safire, "'Voices of Negativism,'" *New York Times*, Dec. 6, 2001.

11. CNN/*USA Today*/Gallup poll, Dec. 14–16, 2001.

12. CNN/*USA Today*/Gallup poll, June 16–19, 2005.

13. CNN/*USA Today*/Gallup poll, April 22–24, 2002.

14. Percentages do not always total 100 percent because of rounding error.

15. See my article, "Public Supports Concept of Missile Defense: But Public Opinion on Issue Is Not Settled," on the Gallup website, Aug. 1, 2001 (www.gallup.com/poll/4753/Public-Supports-Concept-Missile-Defense .aspx).

Chapter Two: Manufacturing Public Opinion

1. David W. Moore, *The Superpollsters: How They Measure and Manipulate Public Opinion in America* (New York: Four Walls Eight Windows, 1992; revised trade paperback edition, 1995).

2. David W. Moore, "How Firm Is the Public's Support for SALT?" *Foreign Policy*, 23 (Summer 1979): 68–73.

3. George F. Bishop, Robert W. Oldendick, Alfred J. Tuchfarber, and Stephen E. Bennett, "Pseudo-Opinions on Public Affairs," *Public Opinion Quarterly* 44, 2 (Summer 1980): 198–209.

4. V. O. Key, *Public Opinion and American Democracy* (New York: Alfred A. Knopf, 1961; reprinted 1964), pp. 79–80n.

5. Elmo Roper, "So the Blind Shall Not Lead," *Fortune*, February 1942, p. 102, cited in George Bishop, *The Illusion of Public Opinion: Fact and Artifact in American Public Opinion Polls* (Lanham, MD: Rowman & Littlefield, 2005), p. 6.

6. Lindsay Rogers, *The Pollsters* (New York: Knopf, 1949), p. 139, cited in Bishop, ibid., p. 7.

7. Daniel Katz, "Chapter 3: The Measurement of Intensity," in Hadley Cantril and Research Associates in the Office of Public Opinion Research at Princeton University, *Gauging Public Opinion* (Princeton, NJ: Princeton University Press, 1944; Port Washington, NY: Kennikat Press, 1972), p. 51.

8. George H. Gallup, "The Quintamensional Plan of Question Design," *Public Opinion Quarterly* 11, 3 (Autumn 1947): 385–393.

9. During the thirteen-year period from 1993 until 2006, while I worked for the Gallup Organization, I had numerous conversations with Alec Gallup, several of which focused on his father's "quintamensional plan."

10. For an account of the experience, as well as a detailed description of the battery of questions and resulting index, see Daniel Yankelovich, *Coming to Public Judgment: Making Democracy Work in a Complex World* (Syracuse, NY: Syracuse University Press, 1991).

11. Daniel Yankelovich, "A New Direction for Survey Research," address to the World Association for Public Opinion Research on receipt of the Helen Dinerman Award, New York, September 1995, *International Journal of Public Opinion Research* 1, March 1996.

12. Gallup poll, March 30–April 2, 2000.

13. Gallup poll, October 6–9, 2000.

14. "Public Opinion about Abortion: An In-Depth Review," at the Gallup website, Jan. 22, 2002, www.gallup.com/poll/9904/Public-Opinion-About-Abortion-InDepth-Review.aspx?version=print.

15. I do not blame the analyst for what I believe is a faulty characterization of the results. When we are forced into the prevailing paradigm, of treating all opinions as though they have meaning, even those that are generated by the selected information we give them, such faulty characterizations are inevitable. It's the paradigm that has to be changed, if polls are to tell the truth about the public.

16. ABC News/*Washington Post* poll, Apr. 21–24, 2005, cited in the *Polling Report*, May 2, 2005.

17. CBS News/*New York Times* poll, March 7–11, 2007, cited on polling report.com (www.pollingreport.com/iran.htm).

18. *Los Angeles Times* poll, Jan. 15–17, 2005, cited in the *Polling Report*, Jan. 31, 2005.

19. Yankelovich, "A New Direction for Survey Research."

Chapter Three: Telling Americans What They Think

1. Eugene Meyer, "A Newspaper Publisher Looks at Polls," *Public Opinion Quarterly* 4 (1940): 239.

2. According to *Safire's New Political Dictionary*, the term "straw poll" originated with author John Selden (1584–1654), who wrote, "Take a straw and throw it up into the air—you may see by that which way the wind is." A straw poll and a straw vote, then, are attempts to see which way the politi-

cal wind is blowing. As O. Henry mused in *A Ruler of Men* (1907), "A straw vote shows only which way the hot air blows." (See http://library.neit.edu/Special/Vote_2004/straw_poll.htm for the etymology of "straw poll—straw vote—straw ballot.")

3. Claude Robinson, *Straw Votes* (New York: Columbia University Press, 1932; New York: AMS Press, 1979): 32–69.

4. For a discussion of the *Digest*'s history, see Robinson, *Straw Votes*.

5. *Literary Digest*, Sept. 10, 1932, p. 3.

6. Hadley Cantril, "How Accurate Were the Polls?" *Public Opinion Quarterly* 1, 1 (January 1937): 103.

7. *Literary Digest*, Nov. 26, 1932, p. 6.

8. Robinson, *Straw Votes*, p. 51.

9. *Literary Digest*, March 1, 1930, p. 3.

10. *Literary Digest*, Nov. 26, 1932, p. 6, emphasis added.

11. *Literary Digest*, Nov. 1, 1924, pp. 5–8; cited in Jean Converse, *Survey Research in the United States: Roots and Emergence 1890–1960* (Berkeley: University of California Press, 1987), p. 119; Robinson, *Straw Votes*, p. 72.

12. James Bryce, *The American Commonwealth*, Vol. 2 (London: MacMillan & Co., 1888).

13. George Gallup and Saul Forbes Rae, *The Pulse of Democracy* (New York: Simon & Schuster, 1940).

14. Robinson, *Straw Votes*, part 2.

15. The references in this chapter to early Gallup Poll data are found in George Gallup, *The Gallup Poll: Public Opinion 1935–1971, Vol. One: 1935–1948* (New York: Random House, 1972).

16. Robinson, *Straw Votes*, part 2.

17. For an overview of the Townsend Plan, see "Agency History—The Townsend Plan,"www.ssa.gov/history/townsendproblems.html. A caution: the history notes that "public opinion surveys in 1935 found that 56 percent of Americans favored adoption of the Townsend Plan." No source is cited, and Gallup did not release a poll on that subject in 1935. When Gallup did poll on that topic, he found overwhelming opposition.

18. Robinson, *Straw Votes*, part 2.

19. For a brief biography of U.S. Surgeon General Thomas Parran Jr., see the Wikipedia entry, http://en.wikipedia.org/wiki/Thomas_Parran,_Jr.#Surgeon_General

20. George Gallup, Question #6, Survey #93, Interview dates 7/28–8/2/37, *Gallup Poll: Public Opinion*, Vol. 1, p. 66.

21. George Gallup, "Government and the Sampling Referendum," *Journal of the American Statistical Association* 33, 201 (March 1938): 131–142.

22. Perhaps the most frequently cited of these critics is Herbert Blumer, "Public Opinion and Public Opinion Polling," *American Sociological Review* 13, 5 (October 1948): 542–549.

23. George Gallup, Question #4, Survey #2, Interview dates 9/18–23/35, *Gallup Poll: Public Opinion*, Vol. 1, p. 3.

24. George Gallup, Question #3a, Survey #3, Interview dates 10/8–13/35, *Gallup Poll: Public Opinion*, Vol. 1, p. 3.

25. Lindsay Rogers, *The Pollsters: Public Opinion, Politics, and Democratic Leadership* (New York: Alfred A. Knopf, 1949), p. 17.

26. Norman C. Meier and Harold W. Saunders, eds., *The Polls and Public Opinion* (New York: Henry Holt & Company, 1949), p. 181.

27. "Man behind the Harris Poll: 'I Elected One President...,'" *New York Observer*, Nov. 14, 1988, cited in David W. Moore, *The Superpollsters: How They Measure and Manipulate Opinion in America*, trade paperback ed. (New York: Four Walls Eight Windows, 1995), p. 78.

28. For a more detailed look at Louis Harris's role in polling history, see chapter 3, "Reinventing the Industry," in Moore, *Superpollsters*, pp. 73–124.

29. See chapter 6, "The Media Pollsters," in Moore, *Superpollsters*, pp. 249–300.

30. Nicholas Von Hoffman, "Public Opinion Polls: Making Their Own News?" *Public Opinion Quarterly* 44, 4 (Winter 1980): 572–573.

31. ABC News website, http://rawstory.com/news/2007/ABC_poll_Bush _hits_new_lows_0115.html.

32. See chart on pollster.com,www.pollster.com/presbushapproval.php.

33. "Poll: Bush Approval Drops to Low of 29%," *USA Today*, July 9, 2007, www.usatoday.com/news/washington/2007-07-09-bush-poll_N.htm. See ibid., for chart.

34. Kathleen Frankovic, "Public Opinion and Polling," in Doris Graber, Denis McQuail, and Pippa Norris, eds., *The Politics of News, The News of Politics* (Washington, DC: CQ Press, 1998), p. 150.

Chapter Four: Inscrutable Elections

1. *Newsweek* poll, Dec. 6–7, 2006, cited in the *Polling Report*, www .pollingreport.com/who08gen3.htm.

2. "Clinton, McCain Face Obstacles on the Road to Nomination," report of *Los Angeles Times*/Bloomberg poll, Dec. 13, 2006, Study #539, based on interviews conducted Dec. 8–11, 2006.

3. CNN poll, conducted by Opinion Research Corporation, Dec. 15–17, 2006, cited in the *Polling Report,* www.pollingreport.com/who8gen3.htm.

4. Fox News/Opinion Dynamics poll, Nov. 16–17, 2005, cited in the *Polling Report,* www.pollingreport.com/who8gen3.htm.

5. Frank Newport, Lydia Saad, Jeffrey Jones, and Joe Carroll, "Where the Election Stands, April 2007: A Gallup Poll Review," April 23, 2007.

6. Gallup poll, July 25–28, 2005, cited in the *Polling Report,* www.pollingreport.com/who8gen3.htm.

7. For all Granite State polls and polls by the UNH Survey Center, consult the website on the 2008 primary (www.unh.edu/survey-center/news/primary2008.html).

8. Scott Helman, "Romney, Clinton Ahead, Vulnerable in N.H. Poll: Race Still Open, Analysts Say," *Boston Globe,* Nov. 11, 2007, www.boston.com/news/nation/articles/2007/11/11/romney_clinton_ahead_vulnerable_in_nh_poll/.

9. Michael Powell and Michael Cooper "For Giuliani, a Dizzying Free-Fall," *New York Times,* Jan. 30, 2008 (www.nytimes.com/2008/01/30/us/politics/30giuliani.html?_r=1&ref=politics&oref=slogin).

10. "Clinton Solidifies Lead among Democrats, Giuliani Still Tops GOP Field," Gallup News Service, May 8, 2007. (www.gallup.com/poll/27523/Clinton-Solidifies-Lead-Among-Democrats-Giuliani-Still-Tops-GOP-Field.aspx).

11. Frank Newport, "Nationally, Choices for Party Nominees Still Wide Open," based on a Gallup poll, conducted Nov. 26–29, 2007 (www.gallup.com/poll/103090/Most-Voters-Decided-Presidential-Candidate.aspx#2).

12. Dan Balz and Jon Cohen, "Clinton and Giuliani Have the Early Edge for '08, Poll Shows," *Washington Post,* Dec. 14, 2006, p. A3, www.washingtonpost.com/wp-dyn/content/article/2006/12/13/AR2006121301593.html.

13. Gary Langer, "Election Polls: What We're After," in "The Numbers— A Run at the Latest Data from ABC's Poobah of Polling, Gary Langer," July 24, 2007, on the ABC website (http://blogs.abcnews.com/thenumbers/2007/07/index.html).

14. Kathy Frankovic, "National Primary Polls Offer Some Insights," Sept. 19, 2007, CBS News website (www.cbsnews.com/stories/2007/09/19/opinion/pollpositions/main3274821.shtml).

15. Gary Langer, "Mind the Gap," in "The Numbers," Dec. 12, 2007, at http://blogs.abcnews.com/thenumbers.

16. "Gallup Daily: Tracking Election 2008 (based on daily polling,

Jan. 27–29)," Gallup website, Jan. 30, 2008 (www.gallup.com/poll/104044/ Gallup-Daily-Tracking-Election-2008.aspx).

17. "A Response from Gallup's Frank Newport," on pollster.com, Feb. 8, 2008 (www.pollster.com/blogs/).

18. "Dueling Gallups," on pollster.com (www.pollster.com/blogs/), Feb. 25, 2008.

19. "AP/Ipsos Poll: Obama Catches Clinton Nationally as He Takes Big Leads among White Men and Liberals," on Ipsos/Associated Press website, Feb. 25, 2008. Also, Robin Toner and Dalia Sussman, "Obama's Support Grows Broader, New Poll Finds," *New York Times,* Feb. 26, 2008 (www.nytimes.com/2008/02/26/us/politics/26poll.html?scp=2&sq=new+york+times+poll&st=nyt).

20. Gary Langer, "+16, +12, +3, +2," The Numbers, Feb. 26, 2008, at http://blogs.abcnews.com/thenumbers/2008/02/16-12-3-2.html.

21. Frank Newport, "Obama vs. Clinton: Two Different Polls," editors blog on Gallup website (www.gallup.com/poll/104545/Obama-vs-Clinton.aspx).

22. See the NCPP website for 2004 Poll Analysis (www.ncpp.org/?q=node/26).

23. Cited by Richard Morin, "Don't Ask Me—As Fewer Cooperate on Polls, Criticisms and Questions Mount," *Washington Post,* Oct. 28, 2004, p. C1 (www.washingtonpost.com/wp-dyn/articles/A3735-2004Oct27.html).

24. Andrew Kohut, "Low Marks for Polls, Media," *Columbia Journalism Review,* January/February 2001.

25. Rich Morin, "Telling Polls Apart," *Washington Post,* Aug. 16, 2000, p. A35.

26. Gallup poll, Sept. 3–5, 1996.

Chapter Five: Misreading the Public

1. For more details, see David W. Moore, "Conflicting Polls Show an Uncertain Public on ANWR," March 8, 2005, at the Gallup website (www.gallup.com/poll/15178/Conflicting-Polls-Show-Uncertain-Public-ANWR.aspx).

2. Gallup poll, March 7–10, 2005, based on sample of 1,004 respondents nationwide.

3. Anne Flaherty, Associated Press, "House Debates Iraq War Policy," *Anderson (SC) Independent Mail,* Feb. 13, 2007 (www.independentmail.com/news/2007/feb/13/house-debates-iraq-war-policy/).

4. All poll results reported here were published on www.polling report.com.

5. CNN/Opinion Research Corporation poll, Jan. 19–21, 2007. N=1,008 adults nationwide. MoE ± 3 (for all adults). Wording: "Suppose Congress considers a resolution which would express opposition to sending more troops to Iraq but would not take specific steps to prevent that from happening. What would you want your members of Congress to do? Should they vote to express support for sending more troops to Iraq [32 percent] or vote to express opposition to sending more troops to Iraq [64 percent]?" Half sample, MoE ± 4.5 Same question asked Jan. 11, 2007.

6. *USA Today*/Gallup poll, Jan. 12–14, 2007, 1,003 adults. "As you may know, the Democrats in Congress are considering passing a resolution to express their opposition to President Bush's plan to send more U.S. troops to Iraq. This resolution, by itself, would not affect Bush's policy, but the Democrats are hoping it will put pressure on him to change his policy. Do you favor [61 percent] or oppose [37 percent] the Democrats in Congress taking *this* action?"

7. *USA Today*/Gallup poll, Feb. 9–11, 2007, 1,006 adults. "Would you favor [51 percent] or oppose [46 percent] Congress passing a nonbinding resolution to express its disapproval of President Bush's plan to send more U.S. troops to Iraq?"

8. *CBS* News poll, Feb. 8–1, 2007. "Do you think Congress should [44 percent] or should not [45 percent] pass a symbolic or nonbinding resolution against sending additional troops to Iraq?" N=578 adults (Form C).

9. Sources of poll:

CNN/Opinion Research Corporation poll, Jan. 11, 2007, 1,093 adults nationwide. "Thinking specifically about the additional troops President Bush plans to send to Iraq, what would you want your members of Congress to do? Should they vote to allow the government to spend money in order to send more troops to Iraq [33 percent], or vote to block the government from spending money to send more troops to Iraq [60 percent]?"

USA Today/Gallup poll, Jan. 12–14, 2007, 1,003 adults. "Would you favor [47 percent] or oppose [50 percent] the Democrats in Congress taking active steps to block the deployment of more U.S. troops to Iraq, such as denying the funding needed to send the additional troops?"

Pew Report, "Broad Opposition to Bush's Iraq Plan," Jan. 16, 2007, http://people-press.org/reports/display.php3?ReportID=301.

CBS poll, Jan. 18–21, 2007. "Which of these comes closest to your opinion? Congress should block all funding for the war in Iraq [6 percent]. OR, Congress should block funding for additional troops being sent to Iraq, but allow funding for troops currently there [50 percent]. OR, Congress should allow all funding for the war in Iraq [8 percent]." Same question asked Feb. 8–11. 2007.

USA Today/Gallup poll, Feb. 9–11, 2007. Would you favor or oppose Congress taking each of the following actions in regards to the war in Iraq: Denying the funding needed to send any additional U.S. troops to Iraq?" Favor [40 percent]; oppose [58 percent]. Same question asked March 2–4 and March 23–25, 2007, with similar results.

ABC News/Washington Post poll, Feb. 22–25. "Would you support [46 percent] or oppose [51 percent] Congress trying to block Bush's plan by restricting funding for the war?"

Associated Press/Ipsos poll, conducted by Ipsos Public Affairs, Feb. 12–15, 2007. "Would you favor [38 percent] or oppose [60 percent] Congress cutting funding for the additional troops President Bush wants to send to Iraq?"

10. Sources:

CBS News poll, April 9–12, 2007. Do you think the United States should [64 percent] or should not [32 percent] set a timetable for the withdrawal of U.S. troops from Iraq sometime in 2008?"

NBC News/Wall Street Journal poll, April 20–23, 2007. "When it comes to the debate on Iraq who do you agree with more: the Democrats in Congress, who say we should set a deadline for troop withdrawal from Iraq [56 percent]; OR, President Bush, who says we should NOT set a deadline for troop withdrawal from Iraq [37 percent]?"

Pew Research Center, March 22–25, 2007. "And thinking about a specific proposal: The Congress is now debating future funding for the war in Iraq. Would you like to see your congressional representative vote FOR [59 percent] or AGAINST [33 percent] a bill that calls for a withdrawal of troops from Iraq to be completed by August of 2008?"

ABC News/Washington Post poll, April 12–15, 2007. "Some people say the Bush administration should set a deadline for withdrawing U.S. military forces from Iraq in order to avoid further casualties. Others say knowing when the U.S. would pull out would only encourage the antigovernment insurgents. Do you yourself think the United States should [51 percent] or should not [48 percent] set a deadline for withdrawing U.S. forces from Iraq?"

11. CBS News, Sept. 17, 2007. "President Bush has proposed reducing the number of U.S. troops in Iraq to pre-surge levels by the summer of 2008. Do you think by next summer, he should remove more troops than that [47 percent], remove fewer troops than that [7 percent], or is that the right amount to remove [29 percent]?" Three percent volunteered "remove all now," 5 percent said "depends," and 9 percent were unsure (www.cbsnews .com/stories/2007/09/17/opinion/polls/main3268663.shtml). See full topline at www.cbsnews.com/htdocs/pdf/sep07b-iraq.pdf.

12. Lydia Saad, "Gen. Petraeus Buys Time for Iraq War, but Not Support: Most Americans side with the level and pace of Petraeus' proposed troop reductions," Sept. 19, 2007 (www.gallup.com/poll/28723/Gen-Petraeus-Buys-Time-Iraq-War-Support.aspx). "As you may know, George W. Bush is adopting General Petraeus's recommendations for future troop levels in Iraq. Based on what you have heard or read about this plan, do you think General Petraeus's plan calls for too few U.S. troops to be withdrawn from Iraq [36 percent], the right amount [43 percent], or too many [9 percent] U.S. troops to be withdrawn from Iraq?" No opinion = 13 percent.

13. CNN/USA Today/Gallup poll, July 7–9, 2003; ABC News/Washington Post poll, July 9–10, 2003.

14. CNN/USA Today/Gallup poll, April 16–18, 2004; ABC News/Washington Post poll, April 15–18, 2004.

15. CNN/USA Today/Gallup poll, June 24–26, 2005; ABC News/Washington Post poll, June 23–26, 2005.

16. Blog on Gallup website posted on July 15, 2003.

17. Poll results can be found on the Polling Report (www.pollingreport .com/health3.htm). The CBS poll was conducted Oct. 12–16, 2007; CNN/ Opinion Research Corporation poll, Oct. 12–14, 2007; USA Today/Gallup poll, Oct. 12–14, 2007; and ABC News/Washington Post poll, Sept. 27–30, 2007.

18. For the complete exchange between Alan Abramowitz and the response by Lydia Saad, see www.pollster.com/blogs/polls_in_the_news/, Oct. 18, 2007.

19. For all poll results on abortion, see the Polling Report (www.polling report.com/abortion.htm).

20. Polling Report (www.pollingreport.com/social2.htm).

21. Michael Faust, "What Gives? Polls Show Differing Results on Amendment Support," Baptist Press, April 8, 2004 (www.bpnews.net/ BPnews.asp?ID=17591).

Chapter Six: Damaging Democracy

1. For accounts of press failure in the run-up to the Iraq war, see Michael Massing, *Now They Tell Us: The American Press and Iraq* (New York: New York Review of Books, 2004), and W. Lance Bennett, Regina G. Lawrence, and Steven Livingston, *When the Press Fails: Political Power and the News Media from Iraq to Katrina* (Chicago: University of Chicago Press, 2007).

2. Massing, *Now They Tell Us,* pp. 41, 44.

3. Cited by Bill Moyers in his speech at the National Conference for Media Reform, January 11, 2007 (www.freepress.net/news/20357).

4. Bennett, Lawrence, and Livingston, *When the Press Fails,* p. 44.

5. Massing, *Now They Tell Us,* p. 46.

6. Bennett, Lawrence, and Livingston, *When the Press Fails.* See especially chapter 3, "None Dare Call It Torture: Abu Ghraib and the Inner Workings of Press Dependence," pp. 72–107.

7. Ibid., p. 75.

8. ABC News/*Washington Post* poll, May 5–6, 2004 (http://abcnews.go.com/images/pdf/953a1PrisonerAbuse.pdf).

9. ABC News/*Washington Post* poll, May 20–23, 2004 (http://abcnews.go.com/images/pdf/955a1BushIraqElection.pdf).

10. CNN/*USA Today*/Gallup poll, May 7–9, 2004.

11. See Wikipedia under "David Koresh" (http://en.wikipedia.org/wiki/David_Koresh) and under Branch Davidian (http://en.wikipedia.org/wiki/Branch_Davidian).

12. CNN/*USA Today*/Gallup poll, April 20, 1993.

13. David W. Moore, "Americans Support Teaching Creationism as Well as Evolution in Public Schools," Gallup News Service, Aug. 30, 1999.

14. George F. Bishop, *The Illusion of Public Opinion: Fact and Artifact in American Public Opinion Polls* (New York: Rowman & Littlefield, 2005), pp. 157–158.

15. Ibid., pp. 11–13, 24–25, 42–44, 61–62.

16. Michael Powell and Michael Cooper, "For Giuliani, a Dizzying Free-Fall," *New York Times,* Jan. 30, 2008 (www.nytimes.com/2008/01/30/us/politics/30giuliani.html?_r=1&ref=politics&oref=slogin).

17. FAIR Alert!, Dec. 21, 2007 (www.fair.org/index.php?page=3234).

18. Susan Page, "Poll: Electability Becoming More Important to Dems," *USA Today,* Dec. 18, 2007 (www.usatoday.com/printedition/news/20071218/a_prezpoll18.art.htm).

19. See the *Polling Report* (www.pollingreport.com/who8gen.htm).

20. See pollster.com (www.pollster.com/08-US-Dem-Pres-Primary.php).

21. Frank Newport, "Nationally, Choices for Party Nominees Still

Wide Open," based on poll conducted Nov. 26–29, 2007, Gallup website (www.gallup.com/poll/103090/Most-Voters-Decided-Presidential-Candidate.aspx#2).

22. Mike Murphy and Mark Mellman, "The Heisenberg Primaries— Candidates and Media Beware: You can't measure what hasn't happened," *Los Angeles Times,* July 5, 2007.

23. Chris Matthews on MSNBC, late evening, Jan. 8, 2008.

24. Scott Althaus, *Collective Preferences in Democratic Politics: Opinion Surveys and the Will of the People* (New York: Cambridge University Press, 2003), p. 9.

Chapter Seven: Uncertain Future

1. The polls and their results are shown in a table below, from pollster .com (www.pollster.com/08-NH-Dem-Pres-Primary.php). I calculated the average based on each poll's results, not weighted for the poll's sample size.

Pollster	Dates	N/Pop	Clinton	Edwards	Obama	Richardson	Obama Margin
Actual Vote Count			39	17	37	5	- 2
Average Poll Results			30	19	38	6	+ 8
Suffolk	1/6–7/08	500 LV	34	15	39	4	+ 5
ARG	1/6–7/08	600 LV	31	20	40	4	+ 9
Reuters/ CSPAN/Zogby	1/5–7/08	862 LV	29	17	42	5	+13
Rasmussen	1/5–7/08	1774 LV	30	19	37	8	+ 7
CNN/ WMUR/UNH	1/5–6/08	599 LV	30	16	39	7	+ 9
CBS	1/5–6/08	323 LV	28	19	35	5	+ 7
Marist	1/5–6/08	636 LV	28	22	36	7	+ 8
Fox	1/4–6/08	500 LV	28	18	32	6	+ 4
Strategic Vision (R)	1/4–6/08	600 LV	29	19	38	7	+ 9
USA Today/ Gallup	1/4–6/08	778 LV	28	19	41	6	+13
Franklin Pierce	1/4–6/08	403 LV	31	20	34	6	+ 3

2. Gary Langer, "New Hampshire's Polling Fiasco," in The Numbers, Jan. 9, 2008, at http://blogs.abcnews.com/thenumbers/.

3. Gary Langer, "The New Hampshire Polls: What We Know," in The Numbers, Jan. 11, 2008, at http://blogs.abcnews.com/thenumbers/. Langer added: "That may seem to put me in the classic definition of a critic: The person who, after watching the battle from the hilltop, rides down and shoots the wounded. The reality is that several of these polls were produced by experienced, consummate professionals; what I really think when I look at their New Hampshire data is that there, but for the grace of God, go I. For all our sakes, we simply need to know what happened."

4. News release, Jan. 14, 2008, received in e-mail from the American Association for Public Opinion Research.

5. David W. Moore, *The Superpollsters: How They Measure and Manipulate Public Opinion in America* (New York: Four Walls Eight Windows, 1992; revised trade paperback edition, 1995).p. 52.

6. See her historical overview, Eleanor Singer, Special Issue Editor, "Introduction: Nonresponse Bias in Household Surveys," *Public Opinion Quarterly,* Special Issue 2006, 70, 5: 637–645.

7. Communication from Howard Schuman on AAPORNET, Jan. 11, 2008.

8. For a review of both studies, see Scott Keeter, Courtney Kennedy, Michael Dimock, Jonathan Best, and Peyton Craighill, "Gauging the Impact of Growing Nonresponse on Estimates from a National RDD Telephone Sample," *Public Opinion Quarterly,* Special Issue 2006, 70, 5: 759–779.

9. See the CPS website (www.census.gov/cps/). See also this website for a discussion of response rates (www.acf.hhs.gov/programs/opre/other_resrch/eval_data/reports/common_constructs/com_appb_popsurvey.htm)

10. Robert Groves, "Nonresponse Rates and Nonresponse Bias in Household Surveys," *Public Opinion Quarterly,* Special Issue 2006, 70, 5: 657.

11. Ibid., 657–664.

12. Ibid., 668.

13. Communication from Howard Schuman on AAPORNET, Jan. 11, 2008 (emphasis added). Quoted with permission.

14. This was the theory advanced by Andrew Kohut at Pew, in his op-ed piece "Getting It Wrong," *New York Times,* Jan. 10, 2008, also mentioned by Howard Schuman in his email to AAPORNET.

15. Scott Keeter, "The Impact of Cell Phone Noncoverage Bias on Polling in the 2004 Presidential Election," *Public Opinion Quarterly* 70: 88–98.

16. Paul J. Lavrakas, Charles D. Shuttles, Charlotte Steeh, and Howard Fienberg, "The State of Surveying Cell Phone Numbers in the United States," *Public Opinion Quarterly,* Special Issue 2007, 71, 5: 841.

17. See a description of NHIS by Stephen J. Blumberg and Julian V.

Lake, "Release of Estimates from the National Health Interview Survey," www.cdc.gov/nchs/data/nhis/earlyrelease/wireless200712.pdf.

18. See ibid. for estimates until 2007; see Lavrakas et. al., p. 843, for projection of cell-phone use by the end of 2009.

19. Scott Keeter, Courtney Kennedy, April Clark, Trevor Tompson, and Mike Morzycki, "What's Missing from National Landline RDD Surveys? The Impact of the Growing Cell-Only Population," *Public Opinion Quarterly*, Special Issue 2007, 71, 5: 772–792.

20. The team of researchers studying national figures consists of Stephen J. Blumberg and Julian V. Luke, "Coverage Bias in Traditional Telephone Surveys of Low-Income and Young Adults," *Public Opinion Quarterly*, Special Issue 2007, 71, 5: 734–749. The team of researchers studying three states consists of Michael W. Link, Michael P. Battaglia, Martin R. Frankel, Larry Osborn and Ali H. Mokdad, "Reaching the U.S. Cell Phone Generation: Comparison of Cell Phone Survey Results with an Ongoing Landline Telephone Survey," *Public Opinion Quarterly*, Special Issue 2007, 71, 5, pp. 814–839.

21. Frank Newport, "Gallup adds cell phones to the mix," *USA Today* blog, Gallup Guru, Jan. 14, 2008, at http://blogs.usatoday.com/gallup/2008/01/gallup-adds-cel.html.

22. "Gallup Adds Cell Phone Interviewing," Jan. 14, 2008, at www.pollster.com/blogs/gallup_adds_cell_phone_intervi.php).

23. Ibid.

24. Rich Morin, "The Pollster Who Answered a Higher Calling," *Washington Post,* June 3, 2002, p. C1.

25. Ibid.

26. Lin Chiat Chang and Jon A. Krosnick, *National Surveys Via RDD Telephone Interviewing vs. the Internet: Comparing Sample Representativeness and Response Quality,* December 2006, manuscript. Received from Krosnick, now at Stanford University.

27. Carl Bialik, The Numbers Guy, "Grading the Pollsters," *Wall Street Journal Online,* Nov. 16, 2006.

28. Numbers taken from the National Council on Public Polls, www.ncpp.org/files/2004%20Election%20Analysis.pdf.

29. Knowledge Networks website, www.knowledgenetworks.com/company/about.html.

Chapter Eight: A New Direction

1. Daniel Katz, "Chapter 3: The Measurement of Intensity," in Hadley Cantril and Research Associates in the Office of Public Opinion Research

at Princeton University, *Gauging Public Opinion* (Princeton, NJ: Princeton University Press, 1944; Port Washington, NY: Kennikat Press, 1972), p. 51.

2. Russell Neuman, *The Paradox of Mass Politics: Knowledge and Opinion in the American Electorate* (Cambridge, MA: Harvard University Press, 1986), pp. 184–185.

3. This is one of the formulations used by Howard Schuman and Stanley Presser in their classic study of question wording and context effects, *Questions and Answers in Attitude Surveys* (New York: Academic Press, 1981).

4. Joseph Carroll, "Public: Iran Poses Greatest Threat to World Stability: Most Americans Not Familiar with New Economic Sanctions against Iran," Oct. 31, 2007 (based on poll conducted Oct. 25–28), Gallup website (www.gallup.com/poll/102463/Public-Iran-Poses-Greatest-Threat-World-Stability.aspx).

5. E-mail communication, Nov. 1, 2007.

6. Adam Clymer, "The Unbearable Lightness of Public Opinion Polls," *New York Times*, July 22, 2001.

7. Susan Page, "POLL: Dems like choices, McCain measures up," *USA Today*, Feb. 11, 2008 (www.usatoday.com/news/politics/election2008/2008 02-11-poll_N.htm).

8. Analysis by Gary Langer, Feb. 3, 2008 (http://abcnews.go.com/Polling Unit/Vote2008/Story?id=4233020&page=1).

9. E-mail from Gary Langer, Feb. 3, 2008. Quoted with permission.

10. Reported by Clark Hoyt, the Public Editor, in "Fuzzy Election Math, Before and After," *New York Times*, Feb. 10, 2008 (www.nytimes.com/2008/02/10/opinion/10pubed.html?_r=2&oref=slogin&oref=slogin).

11. Telephone interview with Alec Gallup, Feb. 1, 2008.

12. Frank Newport, "Putting the New Hampshire Democratic polls under the microscope," in "Gallup Guru" in *USA Today*, Jan. 9, 2008 (http://blogs.usatoday.com/gallup/).

13. Gallup's final figures showed Obama with 41 percent of the vote among likely voters; Clinton, 28 percent; Edwards, 19 percent; Richardson, 6 percent; Kucinich, 3 percent; other, 1 percent; and just 2 percent undecided. See Frank Newport, "Obama, McCain Lead among New Hampshire Voters," www.gallup.com/poll/103600/Obama-McCain-Lead-Among-New-Hampshire-Likely-Voters.aspx, Jan. 7, 2008.

14. Gallup poll, March 15–17, 1996; Gallup poll, Feb. 8–9, 1999.

15. Gallup poll, April 18–20, 1997.

16. Gallup poll, May 2–5, 2005.

17. Lydia Saad, "Tolerance for Gay Rights at High Water Mark," Gallup

website, May 29, 2007 (www.gallup.com/poll/27694/Tolerance-Gay-Rights-HighWater-Mark.aspx).

18. George F. Bishop, *The Illusion of Public Opinion: Fact and Artifact in American Public Opinion Polls* (New York: Rowman & Littlefield, 2005), especially chapter 6, "Ambiguities of Measurement."

19. CNN/USA *Today*/Gallup poll, Q.17, September 2005, #145622.

20. David W. Moore, *The Superpollsters: How They Measure and Manipulate Public Opinion in America* (New York: Four Walls Eight Windows, 1992; trade paperback edition, 1995), p. 357.

21. Daniel Yankelovich, "A New Direction for Survey Research," address to the World Association for Public Opinion Research on receipt of the Helen Dinerman Award, New York, September 1995, *International Journal of Public Opinion Research* 1, March 1996.

INDEX

ABC: polling partner with *Washington Post*, 20, 35, 73; Super Tuesday and, 147–48

ABC News/*Washington Post* poll, 20, 35, 74, 89, 92, 96; Abu Ghraib scandal and, 106–7; problems with poll and, 35–36

abortion: news coverage on, 99; Pew Research poll on, 98–99; poll question order and, 156; poll wording and, 98–99

"abortion pill." *See* RU-486

Abramowitz, Alan, 97

Abu Ghraib prison scandal, 11; ABC News/*Washington Post* poll and, 106–7; Bush administration exoneration and, 108; Iraqi detainees and, 105, 107

Adams, John, 9

Allentown, Pennsylvania, nonresponse problem and, 121

"alternative lifestyle" wording, 153–55

Althaus, Scott, 118

America Speaks! *See under* Gallup, George

American Association for Public Opinion Research (AAPOR), 1, 120, 128

American Institute of Public Opinion, 39

Annenberg School of Communication, 100

Answers in Genesis, 111

Anti-Ballistic Missile Treaty, 15

antimissile program, 14–17

apathy. *See* public ignorance and apathy

arcane issues: respondent knowledge of, 23, 53–54, 82. *See also* public policy

Arctic National Wildlife Refuge (ANWR), 82–85

arms treaty, 22–23

automobile registration lists, 42

Bayh, Evan, 4

Bennett, Lance W., 104, 106